Peter Hay Hunter

After the Exile

A Hundred Years of Jewish History and Literature: Part I

Peter Hay Hunter

After the Exile
A Hundred Years of Jewish History and Literature: Part I

ISBN/EAN: 9783337019501

Printed in Europe, USA, Canada, Australia, Japan

Cover: Foto ©ninafisch / pixelio.de

More available books at **www.hansebooks.com**

To my Father

I DEDICATE THIS BOOK

BY THE SAME AUTHOR

THE STORY OF DANIEL

THIRD EDITION

Uniform with this, Price 5s.

AFTER THE EXILE

AFTER THE EXILE

A Hundred Years of Jewish History and Literature

PART I

THE CLOSE OF THE EXILE

TO

THE COMING OF EZRA

BY

P. HAY HUNTER

MINISTER OF YESTER

OLIPHANT, ANDERSON & FERRIER
EDINBURGH
AND
24 OLD BAILEY, LONDON
1890

TABLE OF CONTENTS.

CHAPTER I.

ISRAEL IN BABYLON.

PAGE

Inscriptions of Cyrus—His origin—Conquest of Media and Persia (550 B.C.)—Threatens Babylon—Condition of the Jewish people in exile—Their material well-being—Their moral sufferings—Influence of the Prophets—Hopes of deliverance—Cyrus 'the anointed of Jehovah'—His first invasion of Babylonia (547 B.C.)—His repulse — Disappointment of the Jews — Their danger — Time of persecution — Cyrus again takes the field — Battle of Routou (539 B.C.)—Defeat and death of Nabonidus—Cyrus enters Babylon . . . 1

CHAPTER II.

CYRUS THE LIBERATOR.

Religion of Cyrus—His worship of the gods of Babylon—His character and policy—Release of the captive peoples—Efforts of the Jews to obtain their freedom—Favour shown them by Cyrus—How to be accounted for—Statement of the Chronicler—Of Josephus—Edict of Restoration—Jewish colouring of the document—Its Reception by the exiles—Disinclination of many to leave Babylon—From worldly motives—From broadened religious views—The Restoration necessary for the mass of the people 28

CHAPTER III.

THE BENE HA-GOLAH.

Younger generation of the Captivity — Its leaders — Zerubbabel the Prince—Appointed pekhah of Judea—The dynastic hope centred in his person—Joshua the High Priest—Number of his followers—Defection of the Levites—Their place in the proposed economy of Ezekiel—His elevation of the Zadokites—Consequent unwillingness of the Levites to return—The Nethinim—Number of the returning exiles—Their comparative poverty—Insistence upon purity of race—Roll of the Congregation—The barriers of caste—Significance of the name 'Bene ha-Golah'—Probable share of the Ten Tribes in the Return 50

CHAPTER IV.

THROUGH THE GATES.

Effects of the Captivity on the outward development of Israel—Advance in knowlege and culture—Trade—Language—Spiritual changes—Hatred of idolatry—Influence of the Great Prophet—Monotheism henceforth rooted in Jewish thought—Limits of Persian influence on Judaism—The Jewish Reformation as pictured by prophecy—The gathering at Babylon—Bounties of Cyrus—Restoration of the Temple vessels—Mingled feelings of the people in quitting Babylon—Lyric of departure—Encouragements of prophecy—The new Exodus (537 B.C.) 76

CHAPTER V.

AMONG THE RUINS.

Homeward journey—Bounds of the new Judea—Gentile neighbours—Condition of the land—Ruins of Jerusalem

—Building of the altar—The first sacrifice—National subscription for the building of the Temple—Arrangements for the work—The site cleared—Ceremony at the laying of the foundation-stone (536 B.C.)—The note of sadness 92

CHAPTER VI.

JEW AND SAMARITAN.

Progress of the work—The Amme ha-Aretz—Origin of the Samaritans—Their religion—Overtures to the colony—Their motives—Parties among the Jews—Reasons for accepting the Samaritan offer—For rejecting it—Decision of the Jewish chiefs—Consequent enmity of the Samaritans—Their intrigues at court—The Edict frustrated—Deadlock in Jewish affairs—The colony forgotten by Cyrus—Discouragement of the people—Their leaders in fault—Decline of popular zeal—Complete stoppage of work in the Temple—Cambyses made King of Babylon (532 B.C.)—Death of Cyrus (529 B.C.)—Accession of Cambyses—Character of that King—His African expedition—Sufferings inflicted on Judea—Cambyses in Egypt—His death (522 B.C.)—Reign of the Magian—Conspiracy of the Seven—Death of the Magian (521 B.C.) . 106

CHAPTER VII.

HAGGAI.

Accession of Darius Hystaspes—His race and lineage—His religious views—Widespread rebellion against his authority—Crisis in imperial affairs—Opportunity of the Jews—The party of prophecy—Their view of the situation—Haggai the spokesman of this party (520 B.C.)—Character and style of his discourses—Their immediate effect—The work resumed—Predicted glory

PAGE

of the new Temple—Zechariah begins his prophetic mission—His social standing—His view of past and present—Vigorous address to the people—Haggai and the priests—Promise of blessing—Haggai and Zerubbabel 133

CHAPTER VIII.

ZECHARIAH.

Opposition of the Samaritans renewed—They denounce the Jews to the Persian governor—Visit of Tattenai to Jerusalem—His report—Building of the Temple continued—Mission of Zerubbabel to the court of Susa—Legend of Zerubbabel—Growing influence of Zechariah—His prophetic standpoint—The seven visions—The abiding strength of Israel—The Jerusalem of the future—Warning to the Jews of Babylon—Message of encouragement to the High Priest—Zechariah as a royalist—As a preacher of morality—Foretells the coming of help from the Golah—Fulfilment of this prophecy—Crowning of the High Priest—Meaning of this symbolic action 152

CHAPTER IX.

THE EDICT OF DARIUS.

Finding of the edict of Cyrus—Generous policy of Darius—Terms of his decree—Authenticity of the document—Effect on Jewish feeling towards the sovereign power—Progress in building the Temple—Arrival of a second deputation from Babylon (518 B.C.)—The question of fasts—Zechariah's treatment of the question—His warning against formalism—Predictions of a better time—Of the future power of Judaism . . . 180

CHAPTER X.

THE SECOND TEMPLE.

Completion of the Temple (516 B.C.)—Ceremony of dedication—Songs of rejoicing—Re-organisation of the priesthood—The passover—Form and dimensions of the second Temple—Its inferiority to the first—Want of the Urim and Thummim—The empty Holy of Holies—Legends of the Ark—Place of the new Temple in popular estimation . . . 194

CHAPTER XI.

THE END OF A DYNASTY.

Blank in Jewish history—Wars of Darius—Marathon (490 B.C.)—Revolt of Egypt—Death of Darius (485 B.C.)—Satrapial system—Place of Judea in the empire—Zerubbabel no longer pekhah—His fate uncertain—Difficulties of his position—Party strifes—Frustration of the dynastic hope—Poets of a lost cause . . . 214

CHAPTER XII.

JOEL BEN PETHUEL.

Accession of Xerxes (485 B.C.)—The Jews seek permission to wall Jerusalem—Again opposed by the Samaritans—Their petition refused—Xerxes invades Egypt (484 B.C.)—Consequent troubles of the colony—Revolt of Babylon—Capture of the city by Xerxes—Fulfilment of prophecy—Invasion of Greece (481 B.C.)—The Solymi—Distress in Judea—Rule of foreign pekhoth—Their exactions—Koheleth—Book of Esther—Prophecy of Joel—His gloomy picture of the time—Lapse of the daily oblation—Joel's call to fast—Prediction of a brighter future for Israel—Of judgment on the Gentiles—Extent of Joel's influence on his contemporaries . 228

CHAPTER XIII.

THE HOUSE OF ZADOK.

Supremacy of the High Priest —The priestly aristocracy— Policy of alliance with the Gentiles—On what grounds defensible—Sentiments of the party of prophecy—Results of the new policy— Outward peace— Lax observance of the Law—Need of a Reformer . . 249

CHAPTER XIV.

THE ISRAEL ABROAD.

Contrast between the Judeans and the Golah—Orthodoxy of the Babylonian Jews—Views as to intermarriage with the Gentiles—Language—Sabbath observance—Advantages of the Golah—Freedom from party strife—Superior culture—Literary activity—Veneration for the Law— Rise of the Sopherim—Their ascendancy . 265

CHAPTER XV.

EZRA THE SOPHER.

Place of Ezra in history—In tradition—Ancestry—Priestly rank—Reputation for scholarship—Distinguished as 'the Sopher'—Reports of the falling away at Jerusalem reach the Golah—Opinions of Ezra—Jerusalem the indispensable centre of Judaism—Complete observance of the Torah impossible elsewhere—Ezra's purpose—Prepares for a mission of reform to Judea—His copy of the Torah—His adherents—Permission of the Persian King a necessary preliminary—Death of Xerxes (465 B.C.)— Accession of Artaxerxes Longhand—His character— Jewish influence at his court—Gentile converts—Ezra and the King—Success of his suit—Extraordinary favour shown to the Jews—Authority granted to Ezra—Its practical restrictions. 281

CHAPTER XVI.

THE NEW EMIGRATION.

Ezra receives his credentials (460 B.C.)—The time apparently unfavourable — Revolt of Egypt — Megabyzus — Ezra's summons to the Golah—Muster on the Ahava—Examination of genealogies—Number of the emigrants—Priestly families—Representative of the house of David—Absence of Levites—Anxiety of Ezra to secure a representation of this order—Settlement of Levites and Nethinim at Casiphia—A deputation sent thither—A number of Levites come into camp—Feeling of anxiety among the emigrants—Dangers of the journey—Ezra's reason for refusing to solicit a military escort—Proclaims a fast—The treasure—Provision made for its safe custody—Departure from the Ahava (459 B.C.)—Resemblance between this and the former emigration—Points of difference—In spirit and temper—In leadership . 302

ERRATA.

On page 17, line 11 from top, "simoom" should be "simoon."
„ 24, „ 4 „ foot, "were" should be "was."

INTRODUCTION.

The century which followed the return of the Jews from the Babylonian Captivity is one of the most important in their annals, and one of the most obscure. This century witnessed the genesis of Judaism, the rise of that religious system from the ruins of ancient Israel. The Assyrian and Babylonian conquests completely destroyed the Israel of old. The state was dissolved; throne and temple fell. The throne was never raised again; the nation never regained political independence, save for that brief space in the days of the Maccabees, which was really a brilliant aberration from the true course of its historical development. The temple was raised again, and round it gathered a community, externally under foreign rule, internally under priestly rule, which henceforth represented the Jewish people. But only a detachment of the people had returned from Babylon; the main body still dwelt in strange lands. And one of the most significant features of the first century of Judaism is the influence exercised on the Israel at home by the greater Israel abroad.

Within these hundred years, the last words of prophecy were spoken, the teaching of Moses was established as the basis of the national life, the first steps were taken towards the formation of a canon of Scripture. Jewish society was moulded into a shape which succeeding centuries modified, but did not essentially change. During this period, the Judea of the days of our Lord came into being. Within this period, the forces which opposed Christ, the forces which rallied to His side, had their origin. This century saw the rise of parties, which afterwards became sects, under the names of Pharisees and Sadducees. It laid the foundations of Rabbinism. It fixed the attitude of the Jews towards the Gentiles.

It put the priesthood on the way to supreme authority. It gave birth to the Samaritan schism.

The history of this period is necessarily a history of tendencies, rather than of events. Judea, as an insignificant province of the Persian empire, had no place in any history save its own. Herodotus never heard of Jerusalem. The circumstances of the Jewish people gave comparatively little scope for the display of great personal qualities or the performance of great exploits by its leading men. All seems on a reduced scale, as compared with the past. Zechariah was the chief prophet, Nehemiah the chief man of action, in an epoch which their contemporaries spoke of slightingly, but mistakenly, as 'a day of small things.' Ezra is the most distinguished figure of the time. In the history of Jewish religion, his name stands rightly between those of Moses and Maimonides. But it is to tradition that Ezra owes his fame. The immediate results of his activity, so far as history records them, were not remarkable.

His work was done for the future, and its issues appeared in the future. A history of this period lacks the interest which is aroused by striking personalities and stirring deeds. The central figure of the time, the true hero of the narrative, is the Jewish people itself—a figure never without its interest, and specially interesting at that special time.

In this volume, the narrative covers three-quarters of the first century of Judaism, and describes how, both within and without Judea, the way was prepared for Ezra's mission of reform. A second volume will treat of that mission and its fruits, and carry the history of Judaism down to the time of the legendary Great Synagogue.

The main authorities for the period are the Books of Ezra and Nehemiah, and those of the last prophets. The view I take of the Books of Ezra and Nehemiah is this, that they originally formed part of the work known as the Book of Chronicles, the author or compiler of which, writing probably in the third century before Christ, incorporated Ezra's and Nehemiah's memoirs, or portions of them, with his narrative. Those passages in the Books of Ezra and Nehemiah which come from the compiler's hand have to be used with a certain degree of caution, partly from the considerable distance of time which lay between the Chronicler and his subject, partly from the very evident prejudices which colour his entire work. But passages which proceed directly from Ezra or Nehemiah, and which stand in their own ungarbled words, may be accepted without hesitation, and have the weight of contemporary evidence. I have purposely avoided touching on questions of Biblical criticism in this book, confining myself to the historical form. The conclusions are given, without statement of the steps by which they have been reached. Hence an appearance, which is only an appearance, of presenting disputed points as if they were undisputed.

One question of criticism, which opens many questions, has to be dealt with in a history of this period—the question as to the nature and extent of Ezra's share in the composition of the Pentateuch. This question is merely touched on in the present volume, and is left for fuller treatment to the second.

Quotations from Scripture are made as a rule from the Revised Version. In some cases, I have given my own translation. In quoting from the Book of Isaiah, I have occasionally followed Dr. Cheyne's rendering.

P. HAY HUNTER.

PASSAGES OF SCRIPTURE CITED OR REFERRED TO

PASSAGES OF SCRIPTURE CITED OR REFERRED TO.

Old Testament.

GENESIS.	PAGE
XIV. 1-15	4
XXIV. 10	64

LEVITICUS.	
XXVI. 36	39

NUMBERS.	
III. 9	310
IV. 2, 3	106
XVIII. 6	310

DEUTERONOMY.	
VII. 1-5	256

II. SAMUEL.	
VII. 13-16	54

I. KINGS.	
V. 11	102
V. 15, 16	103
VIII. 5, 63	195
IX. 21	62
X. 27	121

II. KINGS.	
XVII. 24	107
24	108
27	110
41	110
XVIII. 26	77
XX. 17	210
XXIII. 15-20	110

I. CHRONICLES.	PAGE
II. 55	277
III. 19	52
19	223
19, 20	159
22	306
IX. 3	74
11	256
XVI. 34	104
XXIII. 24	106

II. CHRONICLES.	
II. 10-16	102
III. 4	202
XI. 13	74
XV. 9	74
XXX. 11	109
XXXIV. 9	109
XXXVI. 22	41
23	41

EZRA.	
I. 1	36
1	41
2	32
2	41
2-4	43
3	43
8	52
11	52
11	85
II. 2	64

23

EZRA—(continued.)		EZRA—(continued.)	
	PAGE		PAGE
ii. 20-35	10	vi. 6, 7	184
20-35	93	8, 9	184
59	10	10	186
63	53	11	184
63	208	11	185
64	63	12	183
65	11	13	187
66, 67	63	14	145
66, 67	64	14	184
69	100	15	194
iii. 1	98	17	74
2	52	17	195
7	102	18	199
8	52	20	200
8	106	21	67
9	106	21	201
11	104	22	200
13	106	vii. 6	304
iv. 1	107	6, 28	303
2	111	7	311
3	117	9	303
4	119	10	289
6	229	11	283
7	79	11	294
9	153	12, 21	295
10	108	13	297
11	93	14	299
v. 1	145	14, 25	289
2	142	15, 19	295
3	152	15, 19	297
4, 10	153	21, 22	298
5	154	23	296
6	153	24	298
8	152	25	299
9	154	26	300
14, 15	154	27	295
16	52	27	297
17	154	28	304
vi. 1, 2	181	viii. 1	304
3, 4	87	1-14	305
3, 4	202	2	60
3-5	18	2	306
4	85	3-14	308
4	205	13	305

(EZRA—continued.)	PAGE	NEHEMIAH—(continued.)	PAGE
VIII. 15	60	VII. 12	72
15	305	34	72
16	276	61, 62	72
16	309	65	251
17	10	66	63
17	304	68, 69	63
17	310	68, 69	64
18	303	70	100
18, 19	311	VIII. 2	283
18, 19, 30	315	4, 13	284
18-20	306	7	311
21, 23	314	7, 9	276
22	296	17	69
22	313	IX. 36	236
22, 31	312	37	235
24	306	XII. 4	145
24	315	16	145
26, 27	314	36	284
28, 29	315	XIII. 23, 28	260
31	315	24	268
IX. 1, 2	64		
1	256	ESTHER.	
1	260	I. 1	216
2	255		
2	268	PSALMS.	
8	49	XXIV. 7-10	197
X. 3	279	XLIV. 13, 14	13
10, 16	283	19	24
		22	23
NEHEMIAH.		LXIII. 1	12
		LXIX. 4	25
I. 1	77	7	13
3	217	8, 9	23
II. 1	77	11, 12	13
6	294	20	14
16	68	21	12
20	83	26	24
20	258	LXXIX. 1-3	13
V. 1-13	172	4	13
14, 15	234	4	23
15	235	10	14
VII. 5	68	12	24
6	68	LXXXIX. 19, 20	225
7	64	27-29	225
7	74	34-36	225

PSALMS—(continued.)		ISAIAH—(continued.)	
	PAGE		PAGE
LXXXIX. 38, 39	. 226	XI. 16	. 62
42	. 226	16	. 89
46	. 226	XIII. 2	. 19
XCIV. 20	. 28	3	. 17
CII. 20	. 23	4	. 9
CVI. 46	. 10	4	. 16
CVII. 14	. 28	5	. 16
CXV. 4-8	. 80	6	. 17
CXVIII. 1-4	. 198	15-18	. 24
9	. 120	XIV. 1, 2	. 22
11, 12	. 113	3	. 9
14-16	. 198	4	. 29
19, 20	. 198	23	. 30
26-29	. 198	XXI. 1	. 17
CXX. 2	. 119	2	. 18
5	. 113	10	. 23
CXXII.	. 222	XXII. 6	. 4
4	. 75	XXIV. 1, 6	. 94
CXXIV. 7	. 23	XXV. 6, 7	. 114
CXXVI.	. 88	XXVI. 15	. 121
CXXXII. 1-5	. 226	19	. 84
9, 16	. 227	XXXV. 6	. 89
10, 11	. 227	XLI. 2	. 34
18	. 227	2, 25	. 17
CXXXVI.	. 104	11	. 20
CXXXVII. 1-3	. 12	14	. 23
7	. 94	14	. 38
8, 9	. 24	25	. 16
CXXXVIII.	. 201	25	. 30
CXLVI CXLIX.	. 201	XLII. 6	. 47
CXLVII. 2	. 201	22	. 23
		XLIII. 14	. 17
ECCLESIASTES.		16	. 89
V. 8	. 217	XLIV. 9-20	. 80
8, 9	. 236	28	. 36
		28	. 41
ISAIAH.		XLV. 1, 5	. 17
		2	. 30
VI. 13	. 64	4	. 40
VII. 8	. 71	7	. 82
X. 22	. 62	13	. 34
XI. 12	. 71	13	. 36
14	. 121	13	. 37
15	. 89	XLVI. 1	. 231

ISAIAH—(continued.)		JEREMIAH.	
	PAGE		PAGE
XLVI. 1, 2	30	III. 16, 17	212
11	8	18	71
XLVII. 6	9	IV. 26	94
XLVIII. 1	12	VI. 6	94
10	23	VII. 1-7	170
15	17	VIII. 8	275
21	89	13	94
XLIX. 6	47	IX. 10, 11	96
19	94	11	94
23	121	XXII. 13	10
24	19	XXIII. 7, 8	89
L. 6	13	XXV. 10	96
7	24	11	36
LI. 13	20	XXVI. 18	96
13	24	XXVII. 21, 22	85
14	23	XXIX. 7	14
LII. 8, 9	91	10	36
11	90	11	17
11	91	XXX. 3	71
11	164	6	17
12	89	7	17
12	90	9	54
LVI. 2	269	17	14
3, 6. 7	259	XXXI. 7	62
4	11	29	51
5	83	XXXIII. 10	96
6	22	17	54
7	286	XLIX. 35	4
8	114	L. 2	29
LVIII. 3	13	4	71
6, 7	191	15	25
13	268	17	23
13	269	20	71
LX. 7	206	22	18
10	114	35-37	24
17	121	37	17
LXII. 10	91	38	21
LXIV. 11	206	38	79
LXV. 8	23	43	21
11	3	44	17
LXVI. 1	8	LI. 5	71
7	121	6	164
21	113	11	29

JEREMIAH—(continued.)

	PAGE
LI. 35	25
41	25
42	17
46	9
50	12
LII. 17-23	210

LAMENTATIONS.

II. 1	206
9	54
III. 38	82
IV. 1	96
20	54
V. 2	236

EZEKIEL.

III. 15	10
VI. 14	94
VIII. 1	10
IX. 3	212
X. 18	212
XI. 16	48
XIII. 9	68
XIV. 3	22
XVII. 4	76
XX. 12, 20	268
32	22
34	89
35, 36	51
37	84
XXI. 2	12
XXII. 26	277
XXXII. 25	4
XXXIV. 23	54
XXXV. 5	94
XXXVI. 38	196
XXXVII. 1-14	84
11	14
15-27	71
16	74
22	54
24	54
XLIV. 7-9	61
10	58

EZEKIEL—(continued.)

	PAGE
XLIV. 11, 12	58
13, 14	58
23	27
24	269
XLV. 18	77
XLVIII. 11	58

DANIEL.

II. 4	77
48, 49	11
VI. 10	12
IX. 2	36
X. 2	119

HOSEA.

VI. 2	84

JOEL.

I. 2	234
4, 7	230
9, 13, 16	242
10	240
13	245
14	245
17-20	240
II. 1	247
12	245
13	245
14	242
14	245
15	247
16	245
17	244
17	245
19-24	246
20	233
32	246
III. 3, 6-8	241
4, 5	241
10	246
12-17	247
17	241
19	230

OBADIAH.

	PAGE
10-14	94

MICAH.

	PAGE
II. 12, 13	91
IV. 7	62
VII. 15	89

ZEPHANIAH.

	PAGE
II. 7	62

HAGGAI.

	PAGE
I. 1	52
1	138
2	120
2	141
4	123
4	141
5	141
6	129
6, 9-11	141
6, 10, 11	124
8	142
9	122
9	123
9	141
13	140
13	142
15	142
II. 1	143
3	138
3	143
4	144
5	144
6	144
7	144
8	145
9	145
12, 13	149
14	150
15	150
16, 17	124
16, 19	150
19	148
21-23	139

HAGGAI—(continued.)

	PAGE
II. 22	151
23	151

ZECHARIAH.

	PAGE
I. 1	145
2	147
3	147
4	147
5, 6	147
7	161
8	162
11	162
12	162
15, 16	163
16	162
18-21	163
II. 1, 2	163
4	146
4, 5	164
6, 7	164
11	166
III. 1-5	167
2	167
7	168
8	167
IV. 2, 3	169
6	169
7-10	170
9	104
10	83
10	168
11, 12, 14	169
V. 1-3	173
3	172
4	173
6-8	173
9-11	174
VI. 1-8	174
10	122
10, 11	176
12, 13	177
14	178
15	179
VII. 2	187

ZECHARIAH—(continued.)		ZECHARIAH—(continued.)	
	PAGE		PAGE
VII. 3	189	VIII. 19	13
3, 5	13	19	193
5	190	19	244
7-10	191	20-23	193
9, 10	172		
11, 14	191		
VIII. 3-5	191	MALACHI.	
9-15	192	I. 8	235
10	129	11	294
16, 17	193	II. 7	276

New Testament.

MATTHEW.		THE ACTS.	
	PAGE		PAGE
I. 12	52	III. 2	203
		XXVI. 7	75
LUKE.			
II. 36	74		
		EPISTLE OF JAMES.	
JOHN.			
VII. 35	68	I. 1	68

Apocrypha.

I. ESDRAS.		BARUCH.	
	PAGE		PAGE
IV. 13	159	III. 12	274
29-31	157	IV. 1	274
V. 2, 3	90		
5, 6	159	HISTORY OF SUSANNA.	
6	88	5, 6	10
8	64		
41	63	I. MACCABEES.	
41	73		
66, 67	106	V. 14	109
VI. 29	85	VII. 12	277
		33	186
TOBIT.			
IV. 12	267	II. MACCABEES.	
XII. 15	83	II. 4-8	210

CHAPTER I.

Israel in Babylon.

ABOUT the middle of the sixth century before Christ, Cyrus, King of Elam, began the career of conquest which left him master of Western Asia. Greek writers of history have done full justice to the character of this extraordinary man, but what they tell of his origin, his early adventures and rise to power, is for the most part mere fable. The Cyrus of Herodotus is a fairy prince, the Cyrus of Xenophon a hero of romance; neither can be called historical. Within recent years a new light has been thrown on one of the dimmest figures of the old world by the discovery of contemporary documents, in which the Conqueror of Babylon himself records his victories and the policy of his reign.

For a long time the only known Inscription of Cyrus the Great was that on his tomb at Murgab, in Southern Persia. In the year

1850 there was brought to England a brick found at Senkareh in Lower Babylonia, bearing the legend: *Cyrus, son of Cambyses, king of nations, restorer of Bit-Kitti*—a Babylonian temple. More recently, in the summer of 1879, some Arabs unearthed from the Birs Nimroud what has been described as 'perhaps the most interesting cuneiform document that has been yet discovered'[1]: a broken cylinder of clay, written over from end to end with an account of the taking of Babylon. A second document of scarcely less importance—a small clay tablet, also broken, found in the course of excavations among the Chaldæan rubbish-mounds—contains the annals of Nabonidus, the last native king of Babylon, and recounts the events which led up to the fall of the city.[2]

---

[1] Sir H. Rawlinson, *Journal of the Asiatic Society*, xii. 70.

[2] The Cylinder of Cyrus is barrel-shaped, about 9 inches long, with a diameter of $3\frac{1}{4}$ inches at the end and $4\frac{1}{2}$ inches at the middle. It contained originally nearly 1000 words, in Babylonian cuneiform. Apparently it had been deposited by Cyrus among the archives of one of the great Temples of Babylon, soon after his capture of the city. The Annalistic Tablet measures about 4 inches by $3\frac{1}{2}$ inches, and originally contained two columns of writing on either side. Both Cylinder and Tablet are now in the British Museum. On these Inscriptions, see *Notes on a newly-discovered Clay Cylinder of*

These two sherds of terra-cotta, mutilated and in places illegible as they are, tell enough to reverse many accepted views and to sweep away a host of legends. They explain the swift decline of the power of Babylon. They give an intelligible narrative of the making of the Persian Empire. They show how the warlike Elamite carried his arms from land to land, until at last he crowned his conquests by the greatest of them all, and seated himself on the throne of Nebuchadnezzar.

It appears from the Inscriptions that the founder of the Persian Empire was by no means the parvenu prince described by Herodotus. Cyrus was a king's son, and in early youth, by legitimate succession, himself became a king. From Susa (Shushan) on the Choaspes, his capital city, he ruled over the fertile and populous region lying eastward of the

---

Cyrus the Great, by Sir H. Rawlinson, in *Journal of the Asiatic Society*, xii. 70 ff.; *On a Cuneiform Inscription relating to the Capture of Babylon by Cyrus*, by T. G. Pinches, in *Transactions of the Society of Biblical Archæology*, vii., pt. I., 139 ff.; article by G. Rawlinson, in *Contemporary Review*, 1880, p. 87 ff.; *Cyrus et le Retour de l'Exil*, by Joseph Halévy, in *Revue des Études juives*, I., p. 9 ff.; *Die Kyrossage und Verwandtes*, Bauer, p. 7 ff.

Lower Tigris which bore the name of Elam[1] or Susiana. This realm was one of the most ancient in Western Asia; far back, at the very dawn of history, a King of Elam is found carrying fire and sword up to the borders of Egypt, and undergoing defeat at the hands of 'Abram the Hebrew.'[2] Though overshadowed by the vast empires which rose successively on the Tigris and Euphrates, and forced at times to pay tribute to Nineveh or Babylon, the famed bowmen of Elam[3] had been able to keep their territory intact, and to make their prowess respected by even the greatest of the Assyrian warrior-kings. A native dynasty, however, reigned no longer at Susa. The royal line to which Cyrus belonged was of alien origin, founded by the Persian prince Teispes, son of Achæmenes,[4] of whom little is known beyond the facts that he left his own

---

[1] *An-za-an* in cuneiform. The boundaries of the modern Persian province of Khuzistan or Arabistan are very nearly those of the ancient Elam.

[2] Genesis xiv. 1-15.

[3] 'Elam bare the quiver,' Isa. xxii. 6. '. . . . the bow of Elam, the chief of their might,' Jer. xlix. 35. 'The terror of them was spread in the land of the living,' Ezek. xxxii. 25.

[4] From this shadowy ancestor the dynasty of Cyrus receives the name *Achæmenidæ*.

country, won for himself the crown of Elam, and bequeathed it to his posterity. Cyrus, son of Cambyses, was the fourth of this dynasty. By descent a Persian, by birth and religion an Elamite, with probably Aryan and Semitic blood mingled in his veins,[1] he combined in himself the qualities of both races, and was fitted as no Conqueror had been before to enlist under one banner the forces of a high civilisation and a comparative barbarism, the men of the plains and of the mountains, th worshippers of Bel and of Ormazd.

Nabonidus became king of Babylon in the year 555 B.C. He had raised himself to the throne by conspiracy and murder, and his position at first was insecure. The eastern provinces, Syria and Phœnicia, rose in revolt against the usurper, while the Medes on the north began a harassing warfare and threatened an invasion of Babylonia. This latter danger was averted for the time by an unlooked-for deliverance. In the sixth year of Nabonidus (550 B.C.) Cyrus led his army against Astyages, the Median king. The discontented soldiery

---

[1] *Infrà*, p. 133.

of Astyages mutinied on the eve of battle, seized the person of their sovereign, and delivered him up to the enemy; an act of treason which at once brought about the fall of Ecbatana, the royal city of the Medes. This bloodless victory added Media to the dominions of Cyrus, gave him Ecbatana as a second capital and place of arms, and more than doubled his military strength, for the Medes, one of the most warlike peoples of the day, fought henceforward under the Golden Eagle.[1]

To Nabonidus, relieved from the dread of a Median invasion, these events seemed an interposition of the gods in his favour. He hails Cyrus as the 'young servant' of Merodach-Bel, the patron-god of Babylon. He celebrates the victory over Astyages as if it were his own.[2] Before long it was made apparent how little cause he had for gratitude. The real aim of Cyrus was the overthrow of Babylon, and the construction of a new and still wider empire on the ruins of the old. A far-seeing diplomatist, as well as a skilful

---

[1] The ensign of Cyrus, *Cyropædia*, vii. 1.
[2] Inscription of Nabonidus. Sayce, *Fresh Light from the Ancient Monuments*, 1888, p. 135.

general, he had deliberately laid out the lines
of policy on which success might be won. He
saw around him the peoples restless, the
thrones shaking, and the imperial power held
by the feeble hands of an upstart king. The
Chaldæan armies were no longer the terrible
fighting machine of Nebuchadnezzar's day,
and the martial spirit of the people had been
sapped by wealth, habits of luxury, absorp-
tion in commerce, and the long and peaceful
enjoyment of empire. But the conquest of
Babylon even in its decadence was a gigantic
enterprise, as is very clearly shown by the
fact that Cyrus spent nearly ten years in the
attempt, and only succeeded in the end by
intrigue rather than by arms. His policy was
to strip Babylon of her feudatories and allies ;
to lop off the limbs before striking at the trunk.
One after the other he rallied to his standard
the peoples beyond Tigris, still in their
vigorous youth, unspoilt by luxury, delighting
in war. Within the two years following his
conquest of the Medes he had extended his
sway over the kindred race of the Persians,
from which he himself had sprung. The wild
tribes of Iran had long looked greedily on the

rich Chaldæan plains and cities, and only waited a leader before swooping down like ravenous birds[1] on their prey. This leader appeared in Cyrus. His commanding personality brought and kept together the motley host of Persians, Medes and Elamites, with which he now made ready to deal the first direct blow against Babylon.

Tidings of these hostile preparations travelled swiftly to the Euphrates. The Chaldæan army was massed in Accad or Northern Babylonia under command of the Prince Royal, and prayers and sacrifices for the preservation of the imperial city were offered in the temples of the gods.[2] The people which had invaded so many lands was now in turn menaced with invasion, and however confident the Babylonians might be in their power to beat back the assailant, the mere fact that they were obliged to stand on the defensive was a rude blow to the national prestige, felt not only by themselves but by the races which they held in bondage. The first mutterings of the coming storm—the 'noise of a multi-

---

[1] Isa. xlvi. 11.   [2] Annalistic Tablet.

tude in the mountains,'[1] heard from far—filled these victims of oppression with a furtive joy which became always the more difficult to conceal, as rumour after rumour[2] sped through the land, heralding the approach of war. Of these subject peoples none was so powerfully affected as the Jews, because none had lost so much by their captivity, and none had such good reason to expect its end.

Forty years had passed since the destruction of Jerusalem and the deportation of the great mass of the Jewish people to Babylonia (588 B.C.). During this period, under Nebuchadnezzar and his immediate successors on the throne, the exiles had lived in peace, following without interference their own customs, religious and social. They were certainly burdened with a heavy taxation, and forced to labour without hire in building the temples and palaces of Babylon—a 'hard bondage' from which even old age was not exempt.[3] But such hardships, however severe, were not exceptional; the *corvée* was an institution in all oriental monarchies, and the

---

[1] Isa. xiii. 4.   [2] Jer. li. 46.   [3] Isa. xiv. 3 ; xlvii. 6.

Jews had already become acquainted with it in their own land, under certain of their own kings.[1] The Jewish subjects of Babylon seem, on the whole, to have been treated not unmercifully. Their very weakness disarmed enmity—even called forth the pity of their captors, says a poet of the Exile.[2] They were allowed to form settlements of their own under their own elders and judges,[3] such as those at Tel-Abib, Tel-Melah, and Casiphia[4]; Jewish townships, dotted here and there over the rich Chaldæan cornlands. In these little rural communities the exiles might lead a peaceful, simple family life, among the self-same neighbours who had dwelt beside them in the old home,[5] cultivating their fields, listening to their spiritual teachers, and worshipping the God of their fathers by the river banks, under the open sky. Those of them who lived within the walls of Babylon found a new outlet for their activities in the commerce of that great city, the market of the world; they shared

---

[1] Jer. xxii. 13 ff.
[2] Ps. cvi. 46.
[3] Ezek. viii. 1 ; cp. *Hist. of Susanna*, 5, 6.
[4] Ezek. iii. 15 ; Ezra. ii. 59 ; viii. 17.
[5] See *List*, Ezra ii. 20-35.

freely in the prosperity of the empire, grew rich, built handsome houses, held lands and slaves.[1] High offices under the crown were filled by men of Jewish birth,[2] and there were Jews also among those eunuchs of the palace whose influence at Asiatic courts is often greater than that of ministers of state.[3] This influence might be used in many ways for the benefit of the captive people; and it is possible that their immunity from religious persecution during the first forty years of exile, and the privilege granted them of living after their own fashion and so preserving their organic unity as a nation, were due, at least in part, to the powerful patronage of Babylonian officials who had not ceased to be devout and patriotic Jews.

Such was the outward condition of the Jewish people during the first period of the Captivity. So far as material wellbeing was concerned, they had probably gained by the loss of their liberty, and nothing hindered them from leading a quiet and comfortable life among the Chaldæans, if only they were content to break with their past and give up hope for the

---

[1] Ezra ii. 65.   [2] Dan. ii. 48, 49.   [3] Isa. lvi. 4.

future. But this was impossible for all true Israelites. They could not forget what they had been, or reconcile themselves to be what they now were. They had the means of livelihood in abundance, but to them their drink was as vinegar, their meat as gall.[1] In that land of many streams their spirits fainted for thirst; to them it was a 'dry and weary, a waterless land.'[2] The home-sickness of the people finds manifold expression in the literature of the Exile. 'Let Jerusalem come into your mind!'—so one of the Prophets had adjured his countrymen,[3] and indeed the thought of Jerusalem was with them always. Whether it is Daniel that prays, or Ezekiel that prophesies, the face of the pious Jew is turned towards the Holy City.[4] By the waters of Babylon, they pined for 'the waters of Judah.'[5] The harp that had been attuned to songs of joy was laid aside, and, wandering by the willow-fringed canals, they 'wept, when they remembered Zion.'[6] The anniversary of the destruction of Jerusalem was held as a day of fasting

---

[1] Ps. lxix. 21.
[2] Ps. lxiii. 1.
[3] Jer. li. 50.
[4] Dan. vi. 10 ; Ezek. xxi. 2.
[5] Isa. xlviii. 1.
[6] Ps. cxxxvii. 1-3.

and mourning,[1] a custom which had sprung up spontaneously, for there was no authority to prescribe it, and which kept alive the memory of the national misfortune among the generation born in exile. To think of Jerusalem was to think of the havoc wrought by their enemies—the horrors of the siege and sack, the desecration and burning of the Temple, the blood spilt like water round about the city, the heaps of unburied slain left a prey to the vultures and jackals;[2] and to think of these things was to be filled with hatred and the wild longing for revenge. The Babylonians held them in contempt, and showed it; and the scorn of these idolaters was a ceaseless torture to a proud and sensitive people like the Jews. They exaggerated their own humiliation. Shame covered their face.[3] They were spat upon, laughed at, pulled by the beard; they became a byword among the Gentiles, a subject for the ribald songs of Babylonian revellers.[4] They had to listen in silence to the blasphemous

---

[1] Zech. vii. 3-5; viii. 19; *cp*. Isa. lviii. 3.
[2] Ps. lxxix. 1-3.
[3] Ps. lxix. 7.
[4] Isa. 1. 6; Ps. lxxix. 4; Ps. xliv. 13-14; Ps. lxix. 11-12.

taunts of the heathen, saying, 'This is Zion, whom no man seeketh after'—asking in derision, 'Where is their God?'[1] Each insult, however trivial in itself, was added to the tale of their wrongs, and deep in their hearts they cursed the ruthless power that had trampled on their freedom and their pride. The Prophet had exhorted them to 'seek the peace' of Babylon, to 'pray unto Jehovah for its peace.'[2] They had long ceased to follow such advice. What they sought was the downfall of Babylon; what they prayed for was, not peace, but the sword of vengeance, from whatever quarter it might fall.

That the spirit of the people did not give way utterly under the stress of suffering, that they did not sink into religious indifference and political apathy, was due almost entirely to the influence of the Prophets. There were times of deep dejection, when they felt themselves overborne, heartbroken[3] by calamity, and were ready to cry out that all hope was lost.[4] At such times the Prophets stood between the people and despair. In the visions of Isaiah

---

[1] Jer. xxx. 17 ; Ps. lxxix. 10.
[2] Jer. xxix. 7.
[3] Ps. lxix. 20.
[4] Ezek. xxxvii. 11.

ben Amoz the deliverance of Israel had been foreseen not less clearly than its doom. Jeremiah had spoken that 'amazing word of God'[1] which set a limit to the time of captivity. Ezekiel had sketched the plan of a rebuilt Temple and reconstituted State while as yet both lay in ruins. During the lifetime of the Prophets their words had fallen for the most part on deaf or unwilling ears, but after they themselves had passed away, they found an eager audience among the Jewish exiles on Euphrates. They taught their countrymen how God might be worshipped without temple or altar. They showed them how to remain a nation without prince or land, scattered yet united. They assured them that Israel could not be destroyed, but that Babylon could, and would. And they lit the sacred flame in the hearts of men who took up their message, and made it heard in every Jewish colony over the broad Chaldæan plains. The names of the Prophets who rose up in the latter years of the Captivity, their personal history, are unknown; absorbed in their mission as the

---

[1] Hitzig, *Gesch. d. Volkes Israel.* i. 264.

watchmen of Israel, self-effaced, they were content to be voices and nothing more. But these voices were a power. Now, as at every crisis in the national history, the Prophets stood forth, the true leaders of Israel. They kept the people constantly in mind of their high destinies, and comforted and encouraged them in their darkest hours. To them the triumph of their cause and the overthrow of their oppressors were things assured. They sang the dirge of the King of Babylon, still reigning in his pride. They raised the pæan of victory—'Babylon is fallen!'—while yet the great city stood unassailed. And they showed the people in what direction to look for their Deliverer. It was towards the rising of the sun—to a far country, far as the end of heaven,[1] where Jehovah of Hosts was mustering His legions and preparing His armaments against Babylon.[2] Among the Jewish exiles, enlightened by the prophetic word, the name KORESH[3] passed from lip to lip, and the movements of this new Conqueror were followed

---

[1] Isa. xli. 25; xiii. 5.
[2] *Ibid.*, 4.
[3] The Hebrew form of the native name *Kuras*.

with straining eyes. In default of a national hero they adopted as their champion the Elamite king. This was the *Meshiakh*, the Anointed of Jehovah; the man whom the Lord had consecrated, called and girded, and grasped by the right hand;[1] who was to tread on princes as the potter treads the clay, and to trample kings underfoot, making their sword like the dust, their bow like the driven stubble.[2] He was to come with his wild hordes like a lion from the swelling of Jordan, like the simoon sweeping in from the desert, like a roaring wave of the sea.[3] Before him the hearts of the Babylonians would faint within them and their faces turn pale.[4] It was necessary but scarcely possible for the Jews to dissemble their exultation, their welcome to the enemy of their enemies. For their sakes the Lord was sending to Babylon the chosen minister of vengeance.[5] The 'great day,' the 'day of Jehovah,' the 'expected end,' was drawing nigh.[6] Once again

---

[1] Isa. xiii. 3; xlv. 1, 5; xlviii. 15.
[2] Isa. xli. 2, 25.
[3] Jer. l. 44; Isa. xxi. 1; Jer. li. 42.
[4] Jer. l. 37; xxx. 6.
[5] Isa. xliii. 14.   [6] Jer. xxx. 7; xxix. 11; Isa. xiii. 6.

Elam had gone up, Media had made ready to besiege, and now, after years of waiting and longing, the sound of battle was in the land.[1]

In the month Nisan (March) of the year 547 B.C., the ninth year of Nabonidus, Cyrus crossed the Tigris at the fords of Arbela,[2] eastward of the modern Mosul, and began his first invasion of Babylonia. The Inscriptions do not give so much as a bare outline of the campaign which followed. It may be gathered from them, however, that Cyrus met with a desperate resistance; there is a reference to one Chaldæan vassal-king of those regions who, rather than yield, made of his treasures a funeral-pyre on which he immolated himself and his household. Meanwhile the *fainéant* king Nabonidus lingered in his palace near Babylon, leaving the defence of the empire to his eldest son, the Prince Royal Belshazzar. Whether worsted in battle or, as is more likely, baffled by the difficulties in the way of an invader—the country seamed with water-courses, the numerous fortified towns, the Median Wall

---

[1] Isa. xxi. 2; Jer. l. 22.
[2] Where, two centuries later, Alexander of Macedon overthrew the Empire which Cyrus founded.

—Cyrus was forced to retreat. Next year he renewed the attempt. 'The soldiers of Elam,' says the Annalist, 'marched into Accad'; but again the Chaldæan generals succeeded in barring the way to the capital, and again Cyrus fell back. This check seems to have convinced him that 'the pear was not yet ripe.' For the time he drew off his armies, and turned against another and less formidable foe.

Deep was the disappointment of the Jewish exiles as they watched the tide of war roll back from the Babylonian frontiers. Their promised deliverer had turned from his great venture, Babylon once more had proved her strength, and many were tempted to ask in despair, 'Can the prey be taken from the mighty, or the captives of the terrible one escape?'[1] They had other reasons besides the apparent failure of their hopes for lamenting the repulse of the invading army. They had compromised themselves in the eyes of their masters. They had rejoiced in the peril of the empire; they had 'swung the beckoning hand'[2] to its foes.

---

[1] Isa. xlix. 24.   [2] Isa. xiii. 2.

The feelings and aspirations of a whole people are not easily concealed, however its leaders may counsel and practise the virtue of reticence. It is not necessary to suppose[1] that the Jews had entered into relations with Cyrus, or that the Jewish eunuchs of the palace had furnished him with secret intelligence of what was passing in Babylon. But they had given to Cyrus all they had to give —their goodwill; they had let the signs of it appear; and this was enough to arouse the vindictive fury of the despot who still had them in his power.[2] They were treated no longer with the easy tolerance of contempt, but as covert enemies and a possible danger to the state. Each succeeding year added to the misery of the defenceless people.

Once more the minds of the Babylonians were filled with the terror of invasion. Cyrus had completed his conquest of Asia Minor; Crœsus, king of Lydia, the chief remaining ally of Nabonidus, had been defeated and dethroned. The King of Elam had now over-

---

[1] With Grätz., *Gesch. d. Juden*, ii[b]. 49.; Herzfeld, *Gesch. d. Volkes Jisrael*, 200.
[2] Isa. xli. 11; li. 13.

turned all the thrones save that of Babylon, and none could fail to see that the last stage in the contest for absolute supremacy was at hand. According to the Annalist, Nabonidus had throughout his reign consistently neglected the worship of the gods. But now, under stress of fear,[1] he took all possible measures to appease the offended deities and flatter the angry priesthood, and in this he was seconded by the Prince Royal Belshazzar, whose Inscriptions show him to have been, unlike his father, a most zealous votary of Bel and Nebo.[2] An outburst of fanaticism among the populace, stimulated for their own purposes by the rulers, marked the last days of the Babylonian empire. The people went 'mad upon their idols.'[3] A determined effort was made to stamp out the foreign religions which hitherto had been tolerated on Babylonian soil. From many cities and provinces, near and far, the images of the local divinities were brought to the capital and set up in the temples there; a sign that

---

[1] Jer. l. 43.
[2] See the article *Inscriptions relating to Belshazzar*, by W. St. Chad Boscawen, in *Babylonian and Oriental Record*, Dec. 1887.
[3] Jer. l. 38.

henceforth all exotic worships were proscribed, and all gods of the subject nations degraded before the gods of Babylon. There was nothing tangible to be taken from the Jews; the sacred vessels of their ruined sanctuary stood already in the temple of Bel. But their obstinate clinging to their nationality, their resolute avoidance of all contact with heathenism, the hopes they cherished, perhaps the proselytising energy they displayed,[1] pointed them out for persecution as a singularly impious and rebellious race. The last, the crucial test of the Captivity had come. So far their faith had been tried by the joyous, sensuous rites of Chaldæan idolatry, and the tempting laxity of Chaldæan morals. Many had yielded, either openly abjuring their religion and saying 'we will be as the heathen,'[2] or at least 'setting up idols in their hearts;'[3] but many more, led and inspired by the Prophets, had remained true in spite of all seductions. Now the character of the ordeal was changed. Paganism dropped its blandishments, and showed itself remorselessly cruel to those who

---

[1] Isa. xiv. 1, 2; lvi. 6.   [2] Ezek. xx. 32.   [3] Ezek. xiv. 3.

refused to bow at its altars. The Exile as it neared its close became the furnace of affliction to purge the pure metal from the dross; the threshing-floor to separate the grain from the chaff; the winepress for the crushing of the cluster and the getting of the new wine.[1] Numbers fell away, 'forsook Jehovah' and conformed to idolatry,[2] in order to save their goods or their lives. But the pious remnant of the nation stood firm. They were punished by confiscation of their property, by imprisonment and starvation, even by death.[3] They had to endure the mockeries of their apostate countrymen, who laughed to scorn that 'zeal for the House of Jehovah' with which they were devoured.[4] They were oppressed by the feeling of their own impotence; they felt themselves helpless as scattered sheep before the lions, as a bird entangled in the fowler's snare, as a worm beneath the heel.[5] Every day of their lives was passed in fear; they lay

---

[1] Isa. xlviii. 10; xxi. 10; lxv. 8.
[2] *Ibid.*, 11.
[3] Isa. xlii. 22; li. 14; Ps. cii. 20; xliv. 22.
[4] Ps. lxxix. 4; lxix. 8, 9.
[5] Jer. l. 17; Ps. cxxiv. 7; Isa. xli. 14.

under the shadow of death;[1] at times they even doubted the divine justice, and the cry broke from them, 'They persecute him whom Thou hast smitten!'[2]—as if the chastisement of the Almighty, the sad lot of the exile, were surely sufficient without these added sufferings at the hands of men. But through it all they 'set their faces like a flint'[3] against any concession to idolatry. A frenzied hatred of Babylon, a passionate hope of witnessing its destruction and the sevenfold requital of their wrongs,[4] gave them strength to live through the time of tribulation. The splendid strophes of prophecy inspired and reflected the almost delirious craving for revenge. Their eyes were dazzled with the shining of the sword which was to fall upon their enemies; their minds were filled with visions of massacre and outrage in which neither age nor sex were to be spared.[5] They had their cryptic name for Babylon, as the early Christians had theirs for Rome, and poured forth their maledictions on

---

[1] Isa. li. 13; Ps. xliv. 19. [3] Isa. l. 7.
[2] Ps. lxix. 26. [4] Ps. lxxix. 12.
[5] Jer. l. 35-37; Isa. xiii. 15-18; Ps. cxxxvii. 8, 9.

Sesach[1]—'our blood be upon the inhabitants of Chaldæa!'—'as she hath done, so do unto her!'[2]

It was an unequal contest between the handful of Jewish patriots and the vast forces of the pagan empire,[3] and their rescue did not come too soon. In the seventeenth year of Nabonidus (539 B.C.) the King of Elam once more took the field against Babylon. This time the attack was made from the south-east. An opportune revolt of the southern provinces, probably fomented by Cyrus himself, opened the way for him into the heart of the land. The high-handed policy of Nabonidus, his spoiling of the local shrines to glorify the gods of Babylon, proved fatal to himself; it deeply offended the provincials without reconciling the priesthood, who resented this influx of foreign divinities as an innovation on their ancient modes of worship. Cyrus took full advantage of this state of feeling. To the Babylonians he gave himself out as the vicegerent of Merodach,[4]

---

[1] Jer. li. 41.
[2] *Ibid.*, 35; 1. 15.
[3] Ps. lxix. 4.
[4] Cylinder of Cyrus.

the champion of orthodoxy against an impious king; to the subject nations, as their liberator from the oppressive régime which had robbed them of their dearest treasure—the images of their tutelary gods. On all sides the disaffected subjects of Nabonidus went over to the invader, who passed on at the head of his 'vast army, innumerable, like the waters of a river,'[1] without meeting any serious resistance. The last hope of Nabonidus rested on his Army of the North. In the month Tammuz (June) a pitched battle was fought near Routou, a town in Accad, and ended in the defeat of the Babylonians. A revolution followed at once. The people of Accad rebelled; the cities opened their gates to the enemy; the nobility and priesthood threw off their allegiance, and invited Cyrus to march on the capital. Some days later the victorious army, under a lieutenant of the King, appeared before the walls of Babylon. The collapse of all authority made useless defences which were the wonder of the world; friendly hands threw open the brazen gates, and with-

---

[1] Cylinder of Cyrus.

out a struggle the great city fell. Nabonidus was dragged from his hiding-place, loaded with chains, and thrown into prison, where he died soon after. Four months later Cyrus entered Babylon in triumph, proclaimed himself King of the Chaldæans, and received the willing homage of the people in the palace-halls of Nebuchadnezzar.

CHAPTER II.

Cyrus the Liberator.

IT was inevitable that the Jewish patriotic party, the party of the Prophets, should feel in some degree disappointed with the course of events which brought Cyrus to power, and with the state of matters in Babylon under its new ruler. The 'throne of iniquity'[1] had fallen, their persecutor had miserably perished, their prison-doors were thrown open,[2] and they lived no longer in dread of their lives. But in other points the reality fell short of their expectations. By a timely surrender Babylon had escaped the fate of towns taken after siege and storm. No bands of fierce soldiery dashed through the streets, rioting in carnage; there was no

---

[1] Ps. xciv. 20.
[2] Cylinder of Cyrus:—'the sons of Babylon . . . I opened their prisons.' Ps. cvii. 14:—'He (Jehovah) brought them out of darkness and the shadow of death, and brake their bands in sunder.'

CYRUS THE LIBERATOR. 29

destruction of property, no giving up of the 'golden city'[1] to pillage. 'I entered Babylon in peace,' says Cyrus. His advent marked the end, not the beginning, of a reign of terror; and the inhabitants, thankful for the order and security he brought with him, and appreciating his efforts to gain their goodwill, greeted their Conqueror with effusion —'the men of Babylon, the magnates and the priests, kissed his feet, they rejoiced at his coming, their faces shone.'[2] This was not what the Jews had looked for. They had pictured Cyrus in their minds as the great Iconoclast.[3] By his resistless arm the heathen gods were to be overthrown, the 'vengeance of the Temple'[4] consummated, and all the insults heaped on their religion during fifty years of bondage amply repaid. The sacred images of Babylon, which had so often passed in stately procession through the streets, had been seen in prophetic vision hurled from their pedestals, piled ignomini-

---

[1] Isa. xiv. 4.
[2] Cylinder of Cyrus.
[3] 'Babylon is taken . . . her idols are confounded, her images are broken in pieces' (Jer. l. 2). [4] Jer. li. 11.

ously on carts, and dragged away by the weary ox-teams among the trophies and spoils of the victor.[1] A later day saw all these things accomplished, saw Babylon 'swept with the besom of destruction'[2] and the word of prophecy fulfilled. But in the meantime what the Jewish patriots witnessed was Cyrus—their hero, the man on whom their Prophets had lavished titles of honour, whose mission it was to 'proclaim the name of Jehovah'[3]—publicly ascribing his successes to the favour of the gods of Babylon,[4] offering daily sacrifices on their altars, and restoring and embellishing their shrines.[5]

The hitherto accepted opinion that Cyrus

---

[1] Isa. xlvi. 1, 2.
[2] Isa. xiv. 23.
[3] Isa. xli. 25.
[4] Isa. xlv. 2 :—'I (Jehovah) will go before thee.' Cylinder of Cyrus:—'He (Merodach) bade me take the road to Babylon; like a friend and a comrade he went at my side.' 'It would almost seem,' says Sir H. Rawlinson (*Journal of Asiatic Society*, xii. 83), 'as if the writer on the Cylinder had known the words of Isaiah, and had transferred them to the god of his own religion.'
[5] 'For the work (of restoring the shrine) of Merodach, the great lord, I prepared, and he graciously drew nigh unto me, Cyrus the king, his worshipper, and to Cambyses, my son, the offspring of my heart, and to all my army, and in peace we duly restored its front (in) glory.'—Cylinder of Cyrus.

was an Aryan monotheist, a worshipper of Ormazd, and therefore so far in religious sympathy with the Jews, is seriously shaken if not overthrown by the Inscriptions which record his Babylonian conquest. Even if allowance be made for the fact that these are state documents,[1] and reveal only what the monarch professed, not necessarily what he believed, there still remains the strong probability that Cyrus was not Zoroastrian in creed, but polytheist like his people of Elam. The Cyrus of the Inscriptions is either a fanatical idolater or simply an opportunist in matters of religion. The latter alternative is the more probable. His pious invocations of the Chaldæan divinities, his recognition of Merodach—'the great lord, my helper, who quickens the dead'

---

[1] Cheyne, *The Prophecies of Isaiah*, i. 305. 'It may be said that the writings are not really the composition of Cyrus but of his ministers, and that consequently they throw no light at all on the personal character and disposition of the king. . . . Decrees of such energetic Persian monarchs as Cyrus, Cambyses, Darius Hystaspes, are . . . of weight, and must be regarded as really emanating from themselves They run in the first person; and no subject, whatever his rank, would dare to put into his royal master's mouth any words or phrases which did not express his known mind on the subject-matter of the proclamation."—G. Rawlinson, *Contemp. Rev.* 1880, p. 87.

—as the donor and stay of his throne, mean no more than this, that in order to humour his subjects and confirm his authority over them, he adopted, outwardly at least, their gods as his own. A pagan of the type of Cyrus had no difficulty in admitting the possible co-existence of foreign deities with those of his native land.[1] Each people of his vast composite empire had its own chief god, and it was his policy, as head over each and all, to give that chief god a place in his roomy pantheon. To him, as ruler of Babylon, 'the God of heaven'[2] was Merodach; as ruler of the Persians, Ormazd; as ruler of the Jews, Jehovah.[3]

The system of government which Cyrus

---

[1] 'It is the most characteristic trait of paganism. In that system, the gods of each country exist side by side, and if sometimes they tend to a certain assimilation, they never exclude each other.'—Halévy, *p.* 17. 'The idea that each province has its "geographic god," who requires a certain form of worship, and who takes vengeance if he does not receive the honours consecrated by use, was widespread in ancient times. People who came to a country as inhabitants thought themselves obliged to take the religion of that country.'—Renan, *Histoire du Peuple d'Israël,* ii. 536.

[2] Ezra i. 2.

[3] So Cambyses, the son of Cyrus who followed him on the throne, and conqueror of Egypt, is found paying divine

introduced after his conquest of Babylon bears witness to his religious tolerance, perhaps indifferentism, and at the same time to his rare sagacity and still more rare humanity. His character, as described by the writers of antiquity, was one of singular elevation; gracious, clement and just, treating men as men, and not as mere tools to be used or cast aside, he was a Conqueror of a quite different type from any the world had yet seen. The Persians, says Herodotus,[1] called him the father of his people —a title which certainly had never been given by their subjects to any of the great autocrats of Assur or Babel. He was the 'amiable prince'[2] of the old world. Æschylus calls him 'the generous.' Plutarch declares that 'in wisdom, virtue, and magnanimity he seems to have surpassed all kings.' In his introduction to the *Cyropædia*, Xenophon tells

---

honours to the Egyptian gods; and Darius Hystaspes, a Zoroastrian, in one passage of the Behistun Inscription, ascribes his successes to the aid of ' Ormazd, and the other gods who may exist.'

[1] iii. 89.

[2] *Rex amabilis.* Ammianus xxiii. 6. 'Of his real exploits we know little or nothing, but in what we read respecting him there seems, though amidst constant fighting, very little cruelty.'—Grote, *History of Greece*, iv. 142.

now he was attracted to his subject by finding that this king had been able to govern many nations, differing profoundly from each other, more easily than other kings had been able to govern one ; and that the populations of his empire, no matter how remote, yielded invariably a loyal and cheerful obedience to his commands. To the Hebrew prophets, he was the man raised up in righteousness, the man whom Righteousness called to be her follower ;[1] and the same attribute is claimed for him in the Inscriptions : 'He ruled in justice and righteousness'—'he was righteous in heart and hand.'[2]

No sooner was Cyrus firmly seated on the throne than he set himself to reverse the cruel and senseless measures of his predecessor. The idols of the vassal nations, which Nabonidus had collected in the capital, were restored to their primitive sanctuaries amid the rejoicings of their worshippers. But the new policy of conciliation went even further than this. There were many peoples in Babylonia which had been treated like the Ten Tribes and the Two—torn from

---

[1] Isa. xlv. 13 ; xli. 2.   [2] Cylinder of Cyrus.

their homes, and forced to settle as colonists on foreign soil. With the Assyrian and Chaldæan kings these compulsory migrations had been a favourite method of breaking the spirit of the vanquished, and of preventing revolts and frontier wars. It was a method repugnant to the merciful disposition of Cyrus, as well as to his ideas of good government. The swift dissolution of the Babylonian monarchy warned him against the continuance of a policy which made the sovereign odious in the eyes of his subjects, and planted so many foci of rebellion in the very heart of the empire. He resolved not merely on making an end of this system, but on undoing, so far as possible, the evils it had wrought. In the first year of his reign at Babylon, an edict was issued by which the expatriated peoples were allowed to return home, taking their gods with them. 'I assembled all those nations, and I caused them to go back to their native countries.'[1]

Now was the opportunity of the Jewish people. If only they could gain the king's ear and enlist his sympathy, there seemed no

---

[1] Cylinder of Cyrus.

reason why the favour by which they saw others profiting should not also be extended to them. Their trust in the prophetic word revived. They saw Cyrus 'shepherding' the nations, gathering them as a flock and leading them home; and to them he had been foreshown as the 'shepherd of Israel' who should 'let the captives of Jehovah go.'[1] They saw him restoring the peoples' gods; and it had been said of him that he should speak the word, 'Let the foundations of the Temple be laid.' One prophecy in particular seems to have dwelt in the popular mind, and wrought the conviction that the time of deliverance was at hand. Jeremiah had foretold explicitly that the bondage of the people and the desolation of the land should last for seventy years.[2] Reckoning from the year when Nebuchadnezzar first took Jerusalem and carried away the first company of Jewish captives (606 B.C.), that period had all but elapsed in the first year of Cyrus at Babylon (538 B.C.). Not more than half a century had passed since the destruction of city and temple, but a third genera-

---

[1] Isa. xliv. 28; xlv. 13.
[2] Jer. xxv. 11.; xxix. 10; cp. Dan. ix. 2.; Ezra. i. 1.

tion of the Captivity was living on Chaldæan soil.

The means by which the Jews contrived to make their wishes known to Cyrus, the motives by which he was actuated in granting their suit, have been the theme of many conjectures. It has been suggested that the Jews may have paid their ransom by important services rendered to Cyrus during his campaigns against Babylon. But there is absolutely no record of such services in either sacred or profane history. There is little likelihood that the Jews ever had it in their power to place the Conqueror of Babylon under an obligation. And the Prophet seems to put aside the suggestion —'not for price, and not for reward,' was Cyrus to 'send the exiled ones of Jehovah home.'[1] More plausible is the theory that Cyrus, following the usual course of Asiatic conquest, had already planned an invasion of Egypt, and consequently was not unwilling to see Judea and Jerusalem in the hands of a people bound to himself by ties of gratitude.[2]

---

[1] Isa. xlv. 13.

[2] 'He saw, moreover, that the Jews, if restored from exile, would not only protect the south-western corner of his empire

It is possible that Cyrus may have dreamed of pushing his conquests from the Euphrates to the Nile, and if so it was almost essential that he should be master of the narrow tract between the desert and the sea, for through it went the route which all invaders of Egypt from the north, Assyrian, Scythian and Chaldæan, had taken in turn. Jerusalem, strongly fortified and garrisoned, Judea, inhabited by a numerous and warlike people of proved fidelity to the suzerain power, might have formed an important military outpost of the empire, and a useful base of operations towards the south. But the circumstances of the Restoration make it very doubtful whether Cyrus had any such policy in his mind. The exiles received no permission to repair the dismantled walls of Jerusalem. Of the 'petty folk'[1] of Israel only a

---

from the Egyptians, but would form a base for his intended invasion of Egypt itself.'—Sayce, *Introduction to Ezra, Nehemiah and Esther*, 17. 'It has been suspected that the restoration of the Jews was prompted, at least in part, by political motives, and that Cyrus, when he re-established them in their country, looked to finding them of use to him in the attack which he was meditating upon Egypt. At any rate, it is evident that their presence would have facilitated his march through Palestine, and given him a *point d'appui*, which could not but have been of value.'—Rawlinson, *Monarchies*, iv. 377.

[1] Isa. xli. 14.

fraction returned to their land, contemptible in point of numbers, and unfitted for warfare by a long captivity.[1] Such puny hands could not be counted on to do much in holding the keys of Egypt. If the King of Babylon lost nothing by the transference of this body of Jews from one part of his dominion to another, it is difficult to see wherein he gained.

The exceptional favour with which the Jews were treated by Cyrus must be accounted for on other grounds than those of mere statecraft. That the ruler over myriads of men and hundreds of nations, whose empire extended from the Indus to the Ægean, should have so busied himself with the affairs of a single relatively insignificant people, argues a warm personal interest, from whatever source it sprang. Their religion was the one thing that elevated the Jews above the Gentiles, and gave them, bondsmen as they were, a power and grandeur to which no other nation could lay claim. By their religion, unquestionably,

---

[1] 'And as for them that are left of you, I will send a faintness into their heart in the land of their enemies; and the sound of a driven leaf shall chase them; and they shall flee, as one fleeth from the sword; and they shall fall when none pursueth.'—Levit. xxvi. 36.

they appealed to Cyrus. He was himself an idolater, a worshipper of many gods, and no doubt incapable of fully appreciating or even understanding the pure monotheism of Israel. But it is quite conceivable how a man of noble, generous nature like Cyrus, a man not insensible to higher influences, might be wrought upon by those representatives of the Jewish people who had access to his person, impressed by their fervid sincerity, and impelled to honour the God whom as yet he had not known.[1] There was reality, at least, in this religion of the Jews. Paganism produced no martyrs, but here were men who had clung to their belief in face of bitter persecution, in face of death itself. Here was a faith which had survived the loss of its sanctuary, a Deity worshipped without image or altar, and a downtrodden landless race which claimed to have in its keeping the only true religion. Such ideas were marvellous to the heathen mind; in the case of Cyrus wonder might well grow to admiration; and the discovery that on *him* this strange people had fixed their hopes,

---

[1] Isa. xlv. 4.

that *he* was the man whom they looked upon as their predestined Deliverer, may have prompted him to take up a mission which seemed to be of divine appointment, and which certainly was not unworthy of a great king. Nothing more than this need be read into the pious phrase of the Chronicler :—' Jehovah stirred up the spirit of Cyrus.'[1] How far he was influenced by the Hebrew oracles it is impossible to say. Apparently the prophetic writings which mentioned his name, foretold his victories, and announced his divine calling, were laid before him.[2] But it was impossible for him to test the authenticity of these predictions ; they had

---

[1] 2 Chron. xxxvi. 22 ; Ezra i. 1.
[2] This follows from the clause of the Edict :—' Jehovah, the God of heaven . . . hath charged me to build him an house at Jerusalem ' (2 Chron. xxxvi. 23 ; Ezra i. 2), which is apparently a reference to Isa. xliv. 28. Josephus has the following statement :—' God stirred up the spirit of Cyrus, and caused him to make proclamation through all Asia : " Thus saith Cyrus the King, since the Greatest God hath bestowed on me the kingdoms of the earth, I believe that He it is whom the race of the Israelites doth worship. Moreover, He did foretell my name through the prophets, and that I should build His temple at Jerusalem in the land of Judea." Now this became known to Cyrus by his reading the book which Isaiah left behind him of his prophecy; for this man said that God had thus spoken to him in secret : My will is that Cyrus, whom I have made king over many and great nations, send back My people to their land, and build My temple.

to be taken on trust, at second-hand; and it may be assumed that the living voice had more effect than any documents in swaying his mind. Among his courtiers, his body-guard, his palace-chamberlains, his state officials, were men of Jewish race, ardent patriots, imbued with the prophetic spirit, who found or made the opportunity of interceding for their people with the King. These spokesmen of the Jews have no place or name in their country's annals; they worked behind the scenes. But no sons of Israel ever rendered a more signal service to their nation than the unknown men who pled its cause in the audience-chamber of Cyrus, and won from him the charter of its liberties, the Edict of Restoration.

This was prophesied by Isaiah 140 years before the destruction of the temple. When therefore Cyrus had read this, marvelling at the oracle, a certain impulse (ὁρμή τις) and ambition took hold on him to fulfil the things thus written.' (*Ant.* xi. 1; sects. 1, 2.) Putting aside the statements that Cyrus *read* the prophecies of Isaiah which referred to him by name, and that these were represented to him as having been written two centuries before, there may be some truth in this tradition. The suggestion of Grätz (*Gesch.* ii[b]. 73) that 'one of the (Jewish) eunuchs may have called the attention of Cyrus to the prophecy, *and perhaps even have given it out as being more ancient than it really was*'—is gratuitous and unworthy. The Jewish Restoration was not brought about by a fraud.

This Edict is given by the Jewish Chronicler as follows :—

Thus saith Cyrus, King of Persia: All the kingdoms of the earth hath Jehovah, the God of heaven, given me; and He hath charged me to build Him an House in Jerusalem, which is in Judah. Whosoever there is among you of all His people, his God be with him, and let him go up to Jerusalem, which is in Judah, and build the House of Jehovah, the God of Israel, the God which is in Jerusalem. And whosoever is left, in any place where he sojourneth, let the men of his place help him with silver, and with gold, and with goods, and with beasts, beside the free-will offering for the House of God which is in Jerusalem.[1]

The Edict of Restoration was issued in the first year of Cyrus at Babylon (538 B.C.), and

---

[1] Ezra i. 2-4. This must be taken as a Jewish version of the original decree. In accordance with later tradition, Cyrus is made expressly to identify the 'God of heaven' with Jehovah, and publicly to own the God of the Jews as the bestower of his sovereignty. Evidently the chronicler, without any intention of falsifying the document, has given a Jewish turn to the ascriptions of the heathen king. The phrase in ver. 3— 'the God of Israel, the God which is in Jerusalem'—correctly represents the standpoint of Cyrus, his belief in local divinities. The use of the title 'King of Persia' marks the later date of this version of the edict.

over all the land went the royal heralds proclaiming freedom to the Jews. The patriots who had laboured to bring about this great issue were certainly not slack in rousing their countrymen to take full advantage of the privilege that had been gained. The prophets lifted up their voice in appeals to the national sentiment, recalling the memories of a glorious past, and promising a still more glorious future to the true servants of Jehovah. Many remained deaf to the call. There were those who had virtually discarded their nationality, apostatised from their religion, and become Babylonian in all but blood. To such the Edict of Cyrus was a dead letter, and the word of prophecy an empty sound. There were others for whom the idea of a national restoration had a certain charm, who had bemoaned their exile so long as the prospect of release was shadowy and remote. But now, when deliverance was actually offered, and every man had to choose between going and staying, the reality was found less pleasing than the dream. In Babylon many Jews had risen to affluence and honourable station. There were men of middle age who had been born there, and had never known another home. They were asked, at a time of life when habits are formed and rest is desired, to leave the metropolis of the world for an obscure province, and to exchange the softness and luxury of their present existence for hardship and even danger in what was to them a foreign land. They shrank from the sacrifice. The Captivity produced the earliest examples of a type—the Jewish man of the world who has a certain sentimental pride of race, but otherwise is cosmopolitan. The rich Babylonian Jews no doubt salved their conscience by bestowing gifts on their more self-denying countrymen, and contributing to the fund for rebuilding the Temple, as the royal Edict invited them to do. They gave their money and their sympathy, but nothing more.[1]

There were others among the exiles who also, though for very different reasons, felt no disposition to take part personally in the Return. The same prophets who had laboured to bring about the restoration of their people

---

[1] 'But many stayed behind in Babylon, being unwilling to leave their possessions.' Josephus, *Ant.* xi. 1, 3.

had awakened a spirit in many individuals which made them look on that restoration as unnecessary, so far at least as it concerned themselves. These were the men who had drunk deepest at the well of prophecy, who had risen to the highest conception of God as a spiritual Being, and of Israel as a spiritual community. During the Exile they had seen and suffered much, and their religious views had taken an immensely wider range. In former days it had been generally believed that the religion of Israel was bound up with the body politic, and that the fall of the state must mean the fall of the religion. The state had fallen, the continuity of the national life had been broken, but the religion not only endured —it actually gained in vitality and power. So men came to see that the worship of Jehovah might be independent of the Temple and its ritual, and that a wider Judaism might exist outside the limits of Judea. Even on foreign soil, among foreign peoples, the Jew might still be faithful to his God and his duty, and feel himself as truly in the good keeping of the Eternal as though he dwelt under the very walls of Zion. During the Exile they could not sacrifice, but they learned to pray; and in their sacred literature, the Law and the Prophets, the Histories and the Psalms, they found a 'portable fatherland'[1] of which no force could deprive them, and from which they drew the very life of their souls. Already a consciousness of the high mission of Israel to the Gentile world had formed itself in the best minds of the people. The full scope of the divine purpose for which they had been brought from their own land and scattered among the heathen became gradually apparent. Primarily it had been to effect their own reformation through chastisement, but that accomplished, there still remained a great work for them to do. Theirs it was to prepare for Messiah's coming, to spread the knowledge of the truth, to give light to the nations.[2] The Messianic hope, the sense of Israel's duty to mankind, were shared with the returning exiles by many who stayed behind. They held that each individual Israelite, by leading a pure and holy life among the heathen, might do something towards the conversion of the world and the

---

[1] *Portatives Vaterland.* Heine, *Geständnisse.*
[2] Isa. xlii. 6; xlix. 6.

bringing in of Messiah's kingdom, and thus it was in no wise from religious indifference that they stood aloof from the Return, but rather because they had outgrown, in greater or less degree, the ideas of a circumscribed patriotism and a localised worship.[1] Such spiritual conceptions were as yet beyond the great mass of the people. They needed some tangible guarantee for the fulfilment of the Messianic hope. They needed their native land to assure them that they were still a nation. They needed the Temple, as a pledge of the presence of Jehovah. And for the Jews in Babylonia and Persia and other foreign countries it proved scarcely less of an advantage, as time passed on, that Judea was re-inhabited and the Temple rebuilt. From the far regions in which their lot was cast they looked to Jerusalem as the Holy City of their race and religion, the visible centre and seat of the Theocracy. The exile felt himself no longer a homeless outcast in the world. He had a country of his own. Thither

---

[1] Isa. lxvi. 1. 'Thus saith Jehovah, The heavens are my throne, and the earth is my footstool; what manner of house would ye build for me? and what manner of place for my rest?' *Cp.* Ezek. xi. 16.

he might fare on pilgrimage. There, in hallowed soil, he might hope to find burial.[1] However far he wandered, he 'dragged the lengthening chain' which bound him to the land of his fathers. Henceforth each Israelite had 'a nail in the holy place'[2] — something visible and palpable to lay hold of; a sense of material possession which gave support to the individual, and stability to the whole scattered people.

[1] 'He who is buried in the holy land,' says the Talmud, 'is as though he were buried under the altar.'
[2] Ezra ix. 8.

CHAPTER III.

The Bene Ha-Golah.

WHILE many hung back from cowardice, or love of ease and gain, and some from feelings of exalted piety which placed them in advance of their time, there was a sufficient number of the people who realised the supreme duty of the moment and the great opportunity held out to them by the invitation to return. Of the older generation of the Exile, which had seen and lived through the last terrible days of the Jewish kingdom, only a few came forward in response to the Decree. The work that lay before them was not for broken men, burdened with years, and more sensible of what had been lost than hopeful of what might be regained. It was the youth of the people for the most part that swelled the ranks of the Return. These children of the Captivity felt strongly that the national misfortunes had been brought about by no sin of theirs. It had passed into a proverb with them that 'the fathers had eaten a sour grape, and the children's teeth were set on edge'[1]— *they*, at least, were free from the sense of personal guilt in the matter; *they* had never lain under the curse of Jehovah. They were in the full vigour of manhood, eager to retrieve the past and restore the wreck of their country; and they had the enthusiasm, the buoyant hopefulness, the unselfish devotion to an ideal, which the task required. There were men among them fitted to take the lead in such an enterprise; heads of old historic houses, who were called to the front by inherited tradition not less than by religious zeal. Most of these also belonged to the generation which had risen up in the years of exile. History repeated itself. As the first entrance into Canaan had been reserved for the sons of those who perished in the wilderness, so now the new beginning of the national life was made by new men.[2]

Among the chiefs of the people two person-

---
[1] Jer. xxxi. 29.
[2] The parallel is suggested in Ezek. xx. 35, 36.

ages were conspicuous—Zerubbabel ben Sheal
tiel[1] and Joshua ben Jehozadak; the one representing the royal house of David, the other
the priestly house of Zadok.

Zerubbabel was the grandson of that Jeconiah, the 'winter-king' of Judah, who, after
a reign of three months and ten days, had
been carried away to Babylon and there kept
as a prisoner of state for seven and thirty
years. Zerubbabel—the name is significant;
it means 'Born at Babel'—was *Nasi* or
Prince of Judah, the heir to a fallen throne.
Apparently he held some office at the court of
Babylon, for, like Daniel and his three companions, he bore a Chaldæan[2] as well as a

---

[1] In 1 Chron. iii. 19 Zerubbabel is called son of Pedaiah;
elsewhere, son of Shealtiel: Ezra iii. 2; Hagg. i. 1; Matt. i.
12. He may have been son of Shealtiel by a levirate marriage.

[2] Sheshbazzar. The identity of the 'Sheshbazzar, prince
of Judah,' mentioned in Ezra i. 8, 11, and elsewhere, with
Zerubbabel, is established by a comparison of Ezra iii. 8 *ff.*
with Ezra v. 16. In the former passage it is stated that Zerubbabel, and in the latter that Sheshbazzar, began the building
of the Temple; the natural inference being that these are
different names of the same person. De Sauley (*Étude chron-
ologique des Livres d' Esdras et de Néhémie*, 7) contests this, and
supposes two successive expeditions, the first, which proved
a failure, headed by Sheshbazzar, the second by Zerubbabel.
A similar view is advanced by Rosenzweig (*Das Jahrhundert
nach dem babylonischen Exile*, 32 n.), who makes Sheshbazzar

Jewish name. It is evident that he stood high in the favour and confidence of Cyrus, who made him governor of the new province, under the title *Pekhah* of Judea.[1] This appointment showed either how much Cyrus trusted to the gratitude and loyalty of the Jews, or how little he thought of their power to give him trouble, for he could scarcely be ignorant of the place held by Zerubbabel in the popular regard. It was as if a Russian Czar of former days should have sent a Jagellon to govern Poland, or a German Emperor now should choose a Guelph as viceroy of Hanover. In the eyes of his countrymen, Zerubbabel was no mere official of a foreign state, ruler of a petty district with very limited authority; he was their Prince, the representative of a dynasty which had reigned at Jerusalem for nearly five hundred years, and which had never lost its hold on

---

the Persian plenipotentiary charged with the task of protecting the returning exiles and smoothing over the first difficulties of the new settlement, after which Zerubbabel appeared on the scene as provincial governor. A Jewish tradition (*Jalkut* on Ezra i.) identifies Sheshbazzar with Daniel.

[1] The derivation of the word *Pekhah* is uncertain. Zerubbabel is also called in one place by the Chronicler *Tirshatha* (Ezra ii. 63), a Persian title of a later day.

the affections of the people. The Jews of that day, governed by the tradition of centuries, found it scarcely possible to conceive of a theocracy without a theocratic king—a king of David's line, to which perpetual sovereignty had been promised, and from which the Messiah was to spring. The fall of the throne had seemed to them a calamity second in magnitude only to the destruction of the Temple, and a wail of lamentation followed the last King of Judah into his captivity: 'our king and our princes are among the Gentiles!'—'the breath of our nostrils, the anointed of Jehovah, is taken in their toils!'[1] The hope of a restoration of the Davidic monarchy had never died down in the hearts of the people. It rested on ancient prophecies,[2] confirmed by later seers; by Jeremiah, who had foretold that in the day of deliverance 'Jehovah would raise up David their king;' by Ezekiel, who had declared that Jehovah would not leave His flock without a shepherd, even David His servant.[3] This dynastic hope

---

[1] Lament. ii. 9; iv. 20.
[2] 2 Sam. vii. 13-16.
[3] Jer. xxx. 9; cp. xxxiii. 17; Ezek. xxxiv. 23; xxxvii. 22, 24.

may possibly have been shared by Zerubbabel himself; it was certainly cherished by the patriots who rallied round him.

Joshua was the grandson of the last Jewish High Priest, as Zerubbabel was of the last Jewish king.[1] His grandfather, Seraiah, had fallen in the executions at Riblah after the taking of Jerusalem. His father, Jehozadak, had died during the Captivity. The high priesthood had long been hereditary, and now fell to Joshua by right of birth. His office, though still in abeyance, gave him a unique position among the returning exiles, who felt it a great point gained to have the titular High Priest in the midst of them, ready to resume his sacred functions on their native soil, and to organise the service of the new Temple which was to rise on the ruins of the old. The influence of Joshua may partly account for the large number of priests who joined in the Return. Only four out of the twenty-four divisions of the priesthood are named in the list of emigrants, but these

---

[1] Jeconiah, though not actually the last occupant of the throne, survived by many years his successor Zedekiah, and was looked upon by the exiles as their king.

furnished a contingent of no fewer than 4000 persons, so that a tenth part of the whole community belonged to the sacerdotal order.

In strange contrast to this imposing array of priests was the poor handful of Levites, strictly so called, who gave their support to the undertaking. Of these, only seventy-four came forward in response to the Decree; a singularly paltry representation of the ancient order which had played so important a part in Jewish history. The disparity between their number and that of the priests, their apparent want of patriotic spirit at this great turning-point of the national destinies, their manifest reluctance to quit the homes they had found in Babylon, are among the most curious phenomena of the time, and at once raise the question whether there must not have been some specific reason for this tacit revolt of a whole section of the hierarchy. The explanation is found in the writings of Ezekiel, the priest-prophet of the Exile. The ruling idea with Ezekiel, in his fantastic scheme of a second theocracy, is to have one and one only seat of the sacrificial worship, the centre, spiritually and materially, of the nation. To secure this result he makes elaborate provisions with regard to the priesthood, and among them one which, if put in force, could not but affect directly and most unfavourably the position of the Levites. From the whole tribe of Levi, from the Aaronic branch of that tribe, Ezekiel chooses out one family, the descendants of Zadok, the High Priest of David's time, and confers on that family the exclusive right of serving henceforth the altar of Jehovah. His object in making this selection,[1] which he justifies on the ground that the sons of Zadok had been comparatively faithful and free from idolatry, is evident; he wishes to guard against any attempted revival of the worship of the 'high places' and its consequent abuses, by for ever barring from the priesthood the descendants of those

---

[1] The selection has rather a negative than a positive force, as the priesthood at Jerusalem had been practically in the hands of the Zadokites from the days of Solomon. It is not to be supposed that, as Israel Sack asserts (*Altjüdische Religion*, 31), 'no Aaronic priestly caste had hitherto existed, at least in Judea,' until Ezekiel called one into being by drawing this distinction between Zadokites and Levites. Ezekiel's purpose was to confirm the former in a right already sanctioned by usage, and to secure their exclusive possession of that right in the future by formally setting aside all others of the Aaronidæ as well as the 'Levites.'

who had sacrificed and burnt incense elsewhere than at Jerusalem. Against the Levites Ezekiel shows himself specially severe. They had 'gone astray;' had 'gone away from Jehovah after their abominations;' had 'ministered unto the people before their idols, and been for a stumbling-block of iniquity unto the house of Israel.'[1] Henceforward they were forbidden to 'come near' to Jehovah or to 'do the office' of a priest; theirs were to be the humbler duties of guarding the temple gates, slaying the animals for sacrifice, and acting generally as acolytes to the priests while engaged in their sacred office.[2] Ezekiel declares in so many words that this degradation of the Levites is a punishment for their transgressions: 'Jehovah has lifted up His hand against them': 'they shall bear their iniquity.'[3] But the very terms in which this degradation is pronounced show that, within the prophet's own knowledge, the Levites had in time past performed priestly functions. They had in point of fact officiated in the

---

[1] Ezek. xlviii. 11; xliv. 10, 12.
[2] *Ibid.*, 13, 11, 14. [3] *Ibid.*, 10, 12.

'high places,'[1] and might not inconceivably hope to officiate in the future Temple. If, however, Ezekiel's arrangement was to be carried out, there was nothing very inviting in the prospect held out to them by the Return; they were to be permanently deprived of what they considered a hereditary tribal right, and obliged to perform the menial work of the new sanctuary as servants to the sons of Zadok. Ezekiel's plans for the reconstitution of the priesthood, like his plans for the reconstruction of the Temple, were for the most part quietly set aside as being obviously Utopian. But in this particular instance it chanced that human ambition found itself in unison with the prophet's dream. The sons of Zadok, thus raised above their tribesmen, flocked to the Return in the faith that the Temple would be restored, and with it those honours and privileges of the priesthood which henceforth none else were to share with them. It was found impossible to carry out the prophet's design in its integrity. Members of other priestly houses, which claimed Aaron

---

[1] Baudissin, *Gesch. des Alttest. Priesterthums*, 109; Wellhausen, *Prolegomena*, 128.

but not Zadok as their ancestor, found an entrance into the hierarchy of the second Temple;[1] without such accessions, indeed, the Zadokites would have been too weak numerically for their work. But the sentence of disqualification, while not rigidly enforced against all descendants of Aaron who had served in the Bamoth, was apparently used as a barrier in the case of the Levites; and their unwillingness to descend to a lower status explains why so few of them returned from exile on this and on a later occasion, and even these only under pressure of persuasion.[2]

The position of those Levites who returned to Judea, however unsatisfactory to them at the outset, improved with time. They gained in dignity from the very paucity of their numbers. More honourable functions were assigned to them than those contemplated by Ezekiel; in the hierarchy of the new Temple they formed a second grade, coming between the priests and the classes of choristers and watchmen.

---

[1] Such as the priestly house of Daniel (Ezra viii. 2), belonging to the line of Ithamar. In this case, as doubtless in others, Ezekiel's disqualification was ignored on the strength of more ancient authorities.

[2] Ezra viii. 15, ff.

These latter also rose in importance under the new order of things. At first looked upon as a class distinct from and inferior to the Levites, they seem afterwards to have made good their claim to rank with the ancient Levitical order.[1] No such advance in status was possible in the case of the humblest functionaries of all—those foreign hieroduli who, if Ezekiel's scheme of reform had been adhered to, would have been dismissed from the Temple staff altogether,[2] but whose services were for practical reasons gladly retained. Of these helots of the altar, nearly 400 attached themselves to the emigration: a remarkable trait of heredity, for the captivity of their masters had put an end to their serfdom, and nothing compelled them to take up the lowly duties which their fathers had performed from time immemorial.[3] Thus Joshua found

[1] The 'singers, the children of Asaph' who returned were in number 128; the gatekeepers (*A.V.* 'porters') of the Temple 139. It has been observed that while the classes of choristers and watchmen are in the Memoirs of Ezra and Nehemiah—except in a very few passages, which may be traced to a later hand—carefully distinguished from the Levites, in Chronicles they are classed with the Levites.—Baudissin, *Priesterthum*, 142 ff.

[2] Ezek. xliv. 7-9.

[3] Two classes of these Temple serfs are mentioned—the

himself at the head of a priestly organisation, sadly shrunken in numbers from what it had been in the days of David and Solomon, but still complete in every part, down to the lowest. The hierarchy was ready for the Temple.

Over and over again the Prophets had declared that only a remnant of the people should be spared to see the Babylonian Captivity, and that only a remnant of that remnant should return from it.[1] 'Though thy people, O Israel, were as the sand of the sea,' so Isaiah had warned his countrymen, 'only a remnant of them shall return.'[2] This prophecy, uttered so long before the event, was now strikingly fulfilled. The tribes of Judah and Benjamin in David's reign had numbered about a million souls. Four centuries had passed since that ill-omened census was taken, each multiplying the population. But those two tribes, with that of Levi added, had been so

---

Nethinim or *given ones* ('given' originally as slaves to the Levites), descendants for the most part of those Gibeonites whom Joshua had made to be 'hewers of wood and drawers of water for the house of his God;' and the *children of Solomon's slaves*, descendants of Canaanite bondsmen whom that king had made over in perpetuity to the priesthood (1st Kings ix. 21.)

[1] Isa. xi. 16 ; Micah iv. 7 ; Zeph. ii. 7 ; Jer. xxxi. 7.
[2] Isa. x. 22.

wasted by war, famine, and pestilence, that only some hundreds of thousands went forth into the Babylonian Captivity; and of this relatively small number, which must have vastly increased during the half-century of the Exile, only about forty thousand came back to their native land.[1] 'One of a city, and two of a family'[2]—the forecast was justified by the event. It is said in the Babylonian Talmud that out of the Exile only the chaff returned, while the wheat remained behind. In a limited sense this was true. The Forty Thousand by no means represented the highborn, wealthy, and cultivated classes of Jewish society. They were for the most part poor; so poor that many of them prepared to make the

---

[1] The sum total of the Jews who returned with Zerubbabel is stated at 42,360 in three places:—Ezra ii. 64, Nehemiah vii. 66, and (1st) Apocryphal Ezra v. 41. It is possible that under this summation only *men*—*i.e.*, heads of households—are included; in which case, estimating each household at four or five persons, the aggregate of the Return would be from 150,000 to 200,000 souls. The more modest computation, however, seems by far the more probable. The statement in Ezra ii. 66, 67, Neh. vii. 68, 69, as to the number of beasts of draught and burden in the pilgrim caravan is one indication, among others, in favour of the lesser sum total. Reuss considers a 'number of over 40,000 astonishingly large for a caravan of emigrants.'—*Chronique ecclésiastique de Jérusalem*, 205.

[2] Jer. iii. 14.

long journey homeward on foot, for want of even the humblest beast of burden.[1] But this fragment of Israel, in spite of poverty and paucity of numbers, held fast by the conviction that it stood for the nation—that it *was* the nation. They called themselves, not 'Judah and Benjamin,' but 'the men of the people of Israel.'[2] They ranged themselves under twelve leaders, as though they actually were the Twelve Tribes.'[3] So far from esteeming themselves the 'chaff' or mere residue of the people, they claimed to be the 'holy seed.'[4] Even before the departure from Babylon there appeared among the Jews a tendency, natural enough in the circumstances, but which

---

[1] The whole caravan of upwards of 50,000 persons (slaves included) had with them in all rather more than 8000 beasts of burden; on an average, less than one to each family. Of these only 736 were horses, and 245 sumpter-mules (Neh. vii. 68, 69; Ezra ii. 66, 67). 'Of camels, the animals so especially required by them in the desert journey before them, there were only 435—a very different proportion indeed to that which we read of in Genesis xxiv. 10, when ten camels appear to have been provided for one traveller's use.' Lewis in *Pulpit Commentary, ad loc.*

[2] Ezra ix. 1; Neh. vii. 7.

[3] In Neh. vii. 7 (Apoc. Ezra v. 8), ten chiefs are named together with Zerubbabel and Joshua. In Ezra ii. 2, one of these names has dropped out.

[4] Ezra ix. 2; *cp.* Isa. vi. 13.

afterwards carried them to an unfortunate extreme. For the first time, a line was drawn between those who had a flaw in their pedigree, and those whose purity of race was above suspicion. Each individual who desired to join in the Return had to prove his Israelitish descent, and show his name inscribed in those family registers, those 'books of the generations,' which had been carefully kept during the long years of captivity. This genealogical test was stringently applied. Hundreds came forward claiming to be true Israelites, but unable to substantiate the claim; if not absolutely rejected, they were admitted only on sufferance. A considerable number of priests, whose forefathers had ministered in the Temple without challenge, were now suspended from their office, because no documentary proof was forthcoming of their pure Aaronic descent. The elaborate Roll of the Congregation,[1] drawn up

---

[1] This document is given in three places—Neh. vii., Ezra ii., and Apoc. Ezra v. Nehemiah, according to his own statement, had the original before him when he made his copy. Whether the Chronicler, in Ezra ii., has simply copied Nehemiah's copy, or had access to the original, is uncertain. All three versions vary in regard to names and numbers, as is usual in ancient documents of this description. See Smend, *Die Listen der Bücher Esra u. Nehemia*, 15; *De Wette-Schrader, Einleitung*, i. 386.

in name of the community in the early days of the Return, shows what precautions were taken at the outset against any mingling of foreign or doubtful elements with the seed of Israel. Every man of the Forty Thousand had his place in this official list. It gives the name of family after family, of town after town, and under each the number of its members or burgesses. This was the Golden Book of the new community. To have the name of his forefathers recorded there was counted the highest honour by the Jew of later days. As the English noble is proud of his Norman lineage, as the Spanish hidalgo boasts of his Gothic blood, so the Jewish freeman plumed himself on his descent from one of those heads of houses who came out of exile with Zerubbabel. The men who drew up the Roll of the Congregation had no doubt in their minds that the true Israel was really included within the four corners of that document, and all the rest of the world, Jewish and Gentile, definitely shut out. They could not create a people by such means, but they succeeded in setting up the barriers of caste. When the Babylonian Jews reached Judea, they found numbers of their countrymen dwelling there who had never been carried into captivity at all; the poor of the land, whom the Chaldæans had left undisturbed while they swept away the higher classes of the population. Many of this lowest class, left entirely to themselves after the deportation, had intermarried with the foreigners among whom they lived. Some had fallen into utter heathenism, and were henceforth classed simply among the *Amme ha-Aretz*, the 'peoples of the land.' Others had proved more true to the traditions of their race; and now, when this great body of their countrymen, headed by Prince and High Priest, came back out of exile, they were anxious to throw in their lot with the new community. These people were known as the *Nibdalim*,[1] those who 'separated themselves' from the heathen. They could not be refused a share in the privileges of the Restoration, but they were not received on an equal footing with the families which returned from Babylon. The same thing held true of those who gradually drifted back from Egypt, Phœnicia and other foreign countries, after the Restora-

[1] Ezra vi. 21.

tion had become an accomplished fact. The Babylonian exiles held themselves apart from all such and above them, proudly taking their stand on the Roll of the Congregation, which was preserved in the national archives, and there found, nearly a hundred years after the Return, by the historian who has handed it down to posterity.[1] This was, in their view, the true 'writing of the House of Israel,'[2] and they were the true sons of that House whose names were written there. How tenaciously they clung to this distinction is proved by the collective name they assumed. The immediate result of the Return was to divide the Jewish people into two parts—an Israel at home, and a greater Israel abroad. This latter was properly called *The Golah*[3] or 'Exile,' and from its standpoint the inhabitants of Judea were the *Bene ha-Medinah*, 'children of the province,'[4] or simply 'the Jews.'[5] But the descendants of the Forty Thousand, at least a century after

---

[1] Neh. vii. 5.   [2] Ezek. xiii. 9.
[3] *Golah*—in Aramaic *Galutha*—from a Hebrew root signifying *to make naked*, hence *to strip a land bare of its inhabitants*. The use of the word corresponds to that of the Greek *diaspora* ('Dispersion') used by N. T. writers (John vii. 35; James i. 1).
[4] Neh. vii. 6.   [5] Neh. ii. 16.

the Return, are found still calling themselves *Bene ha-Golah* ('Children of the Exile'), or *Kehal ha-Golah* ('Congregation of the Exile')[1] —an indication that those only were considered true members of the commonwealth whose ancestors had been in the Captivity. *Exile* was still a title of honour at Jerusalem, a mark of superiority, as *émigré* continued to be at the French Court long after the restoration of the monarchy.

The Roll of the Congregation throws very little light on the interesting question as to what part was taken in the Return by other tribes than those of Judah and Benjamin. Two centuries had passed since the destruction of the Northern kingdom and the dispersion of the great mass of its people over the Assyrian provinces. The exile of Ephraim had quite another result from that of Judah, which is explained rather by its beginning so much sooner than by its lasting so much longer. The Ten Tribes and the Two went forth among the heathen at a very different stage of spiritual development, and under very different auspices. During the century and

---

[1] Neh. viii. 17. Smend, *Listen*, 5.

a half that lay between the Assyrian and Babylonian captivities, there had grown up within the community of Judah, corrupt as it was, a true household of faith, sufficiently strong to keep the national religion from perishing with the state, and to carry on the worship of Jehovah after the Temple had fallen, and with it the whole fabric of the Mosaic ritual. But Israel when its exile began had not to anything like the same extent this sound core of religious life, these ideas of a possible worship without holy place or symbol of the divine presence. The sacred literature, the historic past, the definite hope of restoration, above all, the vitalising power of prophecy, which Judah possessed, were wanting to Israel; and hence the same experience which in the case of the one reformed the national religion, in the case of the other practically destroyed it. Here and there individuals or family groups, cast out on the heathen world, might maintain the tradition that they belonged to a people set apart. Here and there the worship of Jehovah might linger on, alloyed more or less with pagan beliefs and practices. But the tendency was towards an ever vaguer recognition and remembrance of Jehovah, and a more complete fusion with the Gentiles, until the Ten Tribes, as a distinct people, virtually disappeared from off the face of the earth. Ephraim had no return from exile like that of Judah. Its polity, once shattered, was never restored; its history, once closed, was never reopened.[1] Yet the Jewish prophets were far from forgetting their kinsfolk or holding them for lost. Their view of the restoration embraced the house of Israel as well as the house of Judah; they delighted to picture the chosen remnant of both peoples, originally one, and now re-united by their common misfortune, laying aside ancient rivalries, and setting forth together from 'the north country' to rebuild the sanctuary and re-possess the land of their fathers.[2] The Return under Zerubbabel may be looked on as a fulfilment of these prophecies, for it is certain that members of the Ten Tribes

---

[1] 'Ephraim shall be broken in pieces, that it be not a people' (Isa. vii. 8).

[2] 'In those days the house of Judah shall walk with the house of Israel, and they shall come together out of the land of the north to the land that I gave for an inheritance unto your fathers.' Jer. iii. 18; cp. Jer. xxx. 3: 1. 4, 20; li. 5; Isa. xi. 12. Also Ezekiel's parable in action—the two sticks joined in one: xxxvii. 15-27.

took part in that undertaking, and came out of exile in company with Judah and Benjamin. The Edict of Cyrus drew no distinction between the Assyrian and Babylonian captivities; the offer of emancipation was freely made to the whole people of Jehovah. There is reason to believe that, after the fall of Nineveh, a number of Israelitish refugees from that city had found a home further to the south, in Babylonia, and so, at a later date, were brought into contact with the exiles of the Two Tribes. They came thus within hearing of the voice of prophecy, within reach of the same influences that wrought the reformation of captive Judah; and there were some at least in whom the spirit of patriotism and the hope of deliverance revived, even after a banishment of two hundred years. It is doubtful whether the Roll of the Congregation contains any statement as to what proportion of the emigrants belonged to the Ten Tribes.[1] The three versions extant of

---

[1] Grätz supposes that the 1254 *Bene Elam* of Neh. vii. 12 are—not a Jewish family, but—a band of Israelitish exiles from the land of Elam; and takes Neh. vii. 34 as meaning 'yet another Elamite family.' (*Geschichte* ii^b. 13n.) Cheyne *Prophecies of Isaiah*, i. 79) also takes *Elam* here as a place-name. The 642 persons referred to in Neh. vii. 61, 62, as unprovided with a genealogy, are thought by Herzfeld to be descendants of the Assyrian Golah. (*Geschichte* i. 453.)

the Roll agree in giving the sum total of the Return as 42,360. But the detailed numbers in all three versions fall short of this sum total leaving unaccounted for about a fourth part of the whole community.[1] There is a general agreement among Jewish commentators that these 11,000 or 12,000 persons, not ranked in the list under any place or family name, were Israelites of the northern tribes.[2] This, however, is a somewhat large assumption, and the difference between the numbers given in the body of the list and the sum total at the end of it is rather to be explained by copyists' errors of omission and enumeration, which are not surprising in a document of this kind. But while it is unlikely that the ranks of the Return were recruited to the extent of one-fourth from the house of Israel, there can be no doubt that not a few of its sons sought and

---

[1] The addition of the figures in Neh. vii. gives 31,089; in Ezra ii., 29,818; in Apoc. Ezra v., 30,143. The author of the last-named Book (v. 41) states that his sum total comprises 'all Israel, from them of twelve years old and upward'—evidently an afterthought, designed to explain away the discrepancy between the detailed numbers and the total.

[2] Wright (*Bampton Lectures: Zechariah and his Prophecies* 279) adopts this view. Neteler (*Die Bücher Esdras, Nehemias u. Esther*, 20) remarks that of the number not accounted for

found admission into the new community.¹ Such were 'the children of Ephraim and Manasseh' of whom the Chronicler makes mention as dwelling in Jerusalem along with the children of Judah;² and the ancestors of that prophetess of the tribe of Asher who witnessed the Presentation in the Temple.³ These adherents from the Ten Tribes were too few to preserve their individuality; henceforth they are known simply as *Jews*. But they were sufficiently numerous to make the twelve-fold leadership and sacrifice⁴ something more than a devout imagination, and their presence in the ranks of the returning exiles was an earnest of greater things to come. For the

---

'one part probably belonged to the other tribes, and returned from the Babylonian Exile along with the tribes of the kingdom of Judah; another part already had its dwelling in the land of Judea, and attached itself to the newly established community.'

¹ Even before the fall of the Northern Kingdom, there had been occasional immigrations of faithful Israelites into the land of Judah—men who were offended by the idolatries of Bethel and sought at Jerusalem a purer worship. See 2 Chron. xi. 13; xv. 9. It is these whom Ezekiel (xxxvii. 16) calls 'the sons of Israel, the associates of Judah.'

² 1 Chron. ix. 3. The list in this chapter is post-exilian; cp. Neh. xi.

³ Luke ii. 36.

⁴ Neh. vii. 7; Ezra vi. 17.

Restoration had its effect on the Assyrian as on the Babylonian Golah. Jerusalem and the Temple were no monopoly of Judah. When Zion had risen again, many sons of Israel in foreign lands looked to it from afar as the sanctuary of their faith; and thus the Psalmist of a later time used no mere figure of speech when he described 'the tribes of Jehovah' as going up to Jerusalem,[1] nor the Apostle when he spoke of 'our twelve tribes instantly serving God day and night.'[2]

---

[1] Ps. cxxii. 4.   [2] Acts xxvi. 7.

CHAPTER IV.

Through the Gates.

A CHANGE had passed over the Jewish people during their captivity, and even those of the new community who had been most faithful to the tradition of national exclusiveness, who had held the heathen most rigidly at arm's-length, did not leave the land of bondage without bearing traces of their sojourn there. On the plains of Chaldæa they had become acquainted with a civilisation more ancient, more complex and advanced by far than their own. They had made considerable progress in culture, in secular knowledge and artistic skill. In the 'land of traffick, the city of merchants,'[1] with its bazaars and banking-houses, whither the trade of the world flowed, the Jewish instinct for commerce and finance awoke and found free play; the Jews ceased to be a purely agricultural people. From the

---
[1] Ezek. xvii. 4.

Babylonians they borrowed their calendar,[1] their alphabet, and, most significant of all, their language. The Jews of the Return were to a large extent bilingual.[2] They had not forgotten their native Hebrew, which was commonly spoken and written, though with some loss of its ancient purity, for long after the Exile. But their enforced intercourse with the Chaldæans had taught them Aramaic,[3] and the convenience of this dialect, which was in some sort the *lingua communis* of the regions from the Euphrates to the Levant, the current

---

[1] 'In Babylon, the people had accustomed themselves to call the months by their Babylonian names. Ezekiel still uses the ancient designations and order of months (*cp.* xlv. 18); but Nehemiah employs the Babylonian nomenclature (Nehem. i. 1, ii. 1). Ezra, retaining the old fashion, gives the number of each month, and omits the name. This also is the practice of the prophet Haggai.'—Friedmann, *The New Year and its Liturgy* (in *Jewish Quarterly Review*, October 1888.) Zechariah uses the Aramaic names of the months. 'The seventh month was instituted the New Year, to commemorate the Return from Exile. . . . . The object of the returned exiles in completely giving up the old calendar may have been to deprive their opponents of every pretext for suspecting that they cherished the design of regaining political independence.'— *Ibid.*

[2] Ewald, *Hist. of Israel*, v. 181.

[3] The *Syriack* of the English Bible, 2 Kings xviii. 26; Ezra iv. 7; Dan. ii. 4. Parts of the Books of Ezra and Daniel are written in Aramaic.

speech of trade and diplomacy, brought it increasingly into vogue among the Jews. It is probable that many of the returning exiles were already more fluent in this *patois* than in their native tongue. The transition had set in which in the end made Hebrew the learned, the sacred language, and Aramaic the vernacular of Judea.

The spiritual transformation of the Jewish people during their captivity was of much greater consequence than those external changes, and with this foreign influences had nothing to do. The generation which went into exile was saturated with idolatry. On all but a few of the best minds of Judah, polytheism had taken a firm hold. The masses had ceased to be worshippers of One God, and moral corruption had attended the decline of the true religion. At various times the state had undertaken to suppress the heathen cults which polluted the land, but these efforts had never more than an apparent success; even while thronging the Temple, the people still clung in secret to their false gods. The silent influence of the Captivity did what no exercise of royal authority had been able to do: it made an end of Jewish idolatry. This reformation, unlike those that had gone before, was complete and final. The tendency to polytheism, which had existed side by side with the worship of the One God from the very birth of the nation, was extirpated within a period of fifty years, and, strangest thing of all, on foreign soil, amid heathen surroundings. It was in the 'land of idols,'[1] the very home of that gross nature-worship by which chiefly their fathers had been led astray, that the Jews came to loathe idolatry as before their fathers had loved it. It was when thrown into closest contact with those orgiastic rites which ministered directly, shamefully, to the senses, that they, a people naturally inclined to sensuality,[2] came to look upon these things as an abomination. The lesson of their past history, read in the light of present experience, and emphasised by the great Prophet of the Exile, brought about this change of heart and mind. The scorching irony of that Prophet, his magnificent ridicule, proved a more deadly weapon than either invective or appeal. That master-picture of

---

[1] Jer. l. 38.
[2] *Projectissima ad libidinem gens.* Tacitus, *Hist.* v. 5.

the manufacture of a god [1]—a picture evidently drawn from the life—was sufficient to convince all thinking men of the intrinsic folly of image-worship, and to make them henceforth look down on heathen nations with sovereign contempt.[2] The same influences which swept away the last trace of idolatry restored the primitive monotheism of the Jewish people, and gave it a broader and firmer basis than it had ever possessed before. After the Captivity, the least enlightened Jew was a monotheist. No contrast could be sharper and clearer than that between the men of Zedekiah's and the men of Zerubbabel's day. Into the Exile there went a generation of heretics; out of it came a generation of devotees. The hidden springs of the movement which resulted in this change are to be sought for within the Jewish people, not without. Under divine guidance they found their own way back to that primitive belief in the divine unity which it was their glory to uphold amid the errors of a heathen world. They certainly did not learn their monotheism from the Persians, a theory

---

[1] Isa. xliv. 9-20.   Ps. cxv. 4-8.

improbable in itself, and made all but impossible by the Inscriptions of Cyrus. If that king himself had been a disciple of Zoroaster, if the Mazdaan doctrines had followed in the wake of his conquering armies, and Mazdaism had been made the state religion of the countries he subdued, then the contagion of ideas, the influence of a pure system of belief over one that had been debased, might explain the revival of Jewish monotheism. But Cyrus, as his Inscriptions show, was not a worshipper of Ormazd; his wars were in no sense wars of religion; the teaching of the Avesta in his day had not passed beyond the limits of Western Iran; and it was not till nearly twenty years after the Jewish Return that a Zoroastrian king sat on the Persian throne. The fable that Zoroaster was a pupil of Daniel at the court of Cyrus is scarcely more absurd than the supposition that the leaders of Jewish thought were indebted for their doctrine to the great prophet of the Aryans.[1] A fanciful

---

[1] 'The child sent into a far country saw other children, who knew more, who lived in more seemly wise; and asked itself, ashamed, Why do not I also know this? Why do not I also live thus? .... Now at length the Jews, acted upon by the purer Persian doctrine, recognised in their Jehovah not

exegesis has found in certain words of Jewish prophets an 'energetic protest' against Iranian dualism.[1] There was no occasion for any such protest, because there was no spread of any such doctrine. Traces of Magian influence on Jewish thought exist in plenty in the Apocrypha[2] and the Babylonian Talmud; in the canonical Scriptures scarcely at all. These 'borrowings from the Gentiles' belong to a later age.[3] The Jews had learned to abhor idolatry long before they became acquainted with the tenets of Zoroaster. It was not the imageless adoration of Ormazd by the Persians, but rather the cruel and lascivious rites with which Bel and Mylitta were worshipped by

---

merely the greatest of all national gods, but God.'—Lessing, *Die Erziehung des Menschengeschlechts*, sects. 38, 39. 'Was it their relations with the least pagan nation of paganism that turned away the chosen people from the sensual cults of Phœnicia?'—Derenbourg, *Hist. et Géog. de la Palestine*, 18.

[1] 'Out of the mouth of the most High proceedeth not evil and good?'—Lam. iii. 38. 'I am Jehovah, and there is none else, that form light and create darkness.'—Isa. xlv. 7.

[2] The Book of Tobit has a strong Persian colouring, but that book is certainly not earlier than the second century B.C.— See Fuller's *Introd. to Tobit*, in *Speaker's Commentary (Apocrypha)* i. 183.

[3] The Jewish doctrine of angels, the idea of the archangelic Seven, were no doubt drawn in part from the Avesta; but so far as Jewish writings produced during or soon after the Exile

the Chaldæans, that opened their eyes to
the guilt of idolatry, and made them recoil
from it in horror. So far as any foreign influence contributed to this reformation, it was
an influence of repulsion, not one of attraction.
What the Jewish community was at the close
of the Exile it had become, not by imitation,
but simply by returning to the 'old ways'
under the strong impulse of calamity. The loss
of earthly greatness and prosperity threw them
back upon their religion, as the one thing that
still remained to them and could never be
taken from them. The loosening of all political ties bound the scattered members of Israel

---

are concerned, their teaching on this point might quite well
be the product of an inner development. (The reference to
the 'seven eyes' in Zech. iv. 10 is a doubtful exception to this
statement; this may, or may not, be an allusion to the Seven
Amshaspands or 'highest spirits' of Zendic mythology—the
'seven holy angels' of Tobit xii. 15. The angelology of
Daniel points to a late redaction of that Book.) So also with
the doctrine of immortality. The astonishingly clear formu-
lation of this doctrine by Zoroaster had no doubt an effect on
later Judaism. But there is no evidence that this doctrine
suddenly gained in clearness among the Jews during or immediately after the Exile. The pious man did not as yet
venture to express the hope of a life after death, of a resurrection of the body. The utmost he hoped for was 'a
memorial in Jerusalem' (Neh. ii. 20), 'a monument within
its walls, which was better than sons and daughters.' (Isa.
lvi. 5).

more firmly together in a brotherhood of faith They felt themselves once more a people consecrated to Jehovah; the 'bond of the covenant,'[1] the national ideal, was restored. Perhaps no change so complete was ever wrought within so short a time.[2] Prophecy pictures it under the figure of a resurrection from the dead. Revival had come on the third day.[3] The dead lived, the dwellers in the dust awoke.[4] The dry bones of Israel came together, the flesh covered the skeleton, the spirit informed the corpse, even as Ezekiel had seen in his Vision of the Valley.[5]

At Babylon, in the first month of the second year of Cyrus (537 B.C.), the Children of the Exile gathered themselves together, and prepared to set out on the long journey homeward. The forethought and generosity of Cyrus, his thorough interest in the fortunes

---

[1] Ezek. xx. 37.

[2] 'The whole history of that time,' says a Jewish writer, 'seems to us even incomprehensible. We, who see before us everywhere in nature as in human life an equable, continuous progression, can only marvel at the sudden transformation which passed over the Hebrew people during the brief period of their sojourn in Chaldæa.'—Bloch, *Studien,* 47.

[3] Hosea vi. 2. [4] Isa. xxvi. 19. [5] Ezek. xxxvii. 1-14.

of his Jewish subjects, were shown by the favours he bestowed on them at parting. He gave them the vessels of their Temple, which Nebuchadnezzar had preserved as trophies in the house of Bel, and which were now brought forth and handed over to Zerubbabel by the royal treasurer[1]—a gift worthy of a king, for these censers and chalices, goblets, basins and salvers, all of gold and silver, were very numerous[2] and of great intrinsic value. He gave them, or undertook to give, a grant in aid of the rebuilding of the Temple, chargeable on the revenues of the Syrian province.[3] He gave them finally an escort of a thousand troopers,[4]

---

[1] A remarkable fulfilment of prophecy: 'Thus saith Jehovah of Hosts, concerning the vessels that remain in the house of Jehovah . . . they shall be carried to Babylon, and there shall they be until the day that I visit them, saith Jehovah; then will I bring them up, and restore them to this place' (Jer. xxvii. 21, 22).

[2] Their total is given by the Chronicler (Ezra i. 11) as 5400. Keil (*Commentary ad loc.*) suspects an error in the text, which would reduce the total—suspiciously large—to 2500.

[3] Ezra vi. 4; Apoc. Ezra vi. 29; Josephus, *Ant.* xi. 1, 3.

[4] This, with other particulars not given in the Book of Ezra, is found in Apoc. Ezra v. 1-6, perhaps the only passage of real historical value in that Book. These six verses are evidently a Greek translation of a Hebrew original, and it is possible that that original may have been a short section which has dropped from the Book of Ezra, between chaps. i. and ii. The author of Apoc. Ezra has here changed the name *Cyrus* into *Darius*. (Bertheau-Ryssel, *Esra, Nechemia u. Ester,*

without which their journey through the desert, laden as they were with treasure, and wanting the means of self-defence, would have been dangerous in the extreme.

It was with a strange mingling of sadness and exultation that the Children of the Exile looked out on the prospect before them. They were leaving the place of their birth, the graves of their fathers, the homesteads they had built, the gardens they had planted, the fields they had tilled. They were bidding farewell to many of their kinsfolk, who had chosen the safer part, and were not to travel with them. They were quitting a land of plenty, where, under a friendly government, they might have dwelt in peace, no man making them afraid. Even the enthusiasm of the hour could not quite banish the natural feelings of regret and anxiety. They were painfully aware of their own weakness, the scantiness of their numbers, their complete dependence on the favour of a Gentile king. The very gifts and concessions of Cyrus carried with them a certain humiliation. It

---

in *Kurzgef. exeg. Handbuch zum A. T.*, 12; Fritzsche, *Handbuch zu den Apok. des. A. T.* i. 33.)

was humbling to Jewish pride that they had to sue for the leave of a foreign ruler before one course of the Temple walls could be laid upon another. It was humbling to have the form and dimensions of their holy place determined for them, as they were in a royal rescript addressed to Zerubbabel,[1] and all the more that they could not complain of this, since a large proportion of the expense of building was to be met from the king's privy purse. And among those sacred furnishings of the Temple which the munificence of Cyrus had restored to them, one thing was wanting, the most precious of all—the Ark of Jehovah,[2] the visible symbol of the divine presence, now lost and never recovered. All these things explain the blending of tears and triumph, of melancholy and hope, which makes the verses of the exile-poet such a perfect embodiment of the feeling of the people :—

> 'When Jehovah turned again the captivity of Zion,
> We were like men that dream.
> Then was our mouth filled with laughter,
> And our tongue with singing. . . .

---

[1] Ezra vi. 3, 4.   [2] *Infrà*, p. 209.

They that sow in tears shall reap in joy.
Though he goeth on his way weeping, bearing forth the seed,
He shall come again rejoicing, bringing with him his sheaves.'[1]

There was one memorable event in the past history of Israel which the circumstances of the present brought vividly before the popular mind. This month in which they were setting forth from Babylon—the 'month of opening,' Nisan (March)[2]—was the same in which their forefathers had gone up out of Egypt nearly a thousand years before. The coincidence was seized upon as an omen. The parallel between the First and the Second Exodus was too obvious to be missed; it had been repeatedly suggested and enlarged upon by the prophets, and had been made the theme of promises and predictions which were fitted to embolden the most timid and to cheer the most despondent. Now, as then, their deliverance had been marked by the overthrow of their enemies; as Pharaoh and his host had perished, so had the power of Babylon passed into other hands. Now, as then, they were going forth enriched with the gifts of the Gentiles. Now, as then, Jehovah was to pass at the head of his

---

[1] Ps. cxxvi. [2] Apoc. Ezra, v. 6.

ransomed people,[1] and 'with a mighty hand and a stretched-out arm'[2] to bring them on their way. Jehovah was to shake his hand over the River, the Euphrates, as before over the Red Sea, and part its waters for their crossing.[3] The desert that lay between Babylon and Judea was to see repeated the wonders of the wilderness of Sinai.[4] Once more a highway was to be made through the barren waste, 'like as there was for Israel in the day that he came up out of Egypt.'[5] Once more water was to gush from the rock or spring from the sands.[6] The glory of this new redemption was to surpass all that had gone before; no longer would men say, 'As Jehovah liveth, which brought up the children of Israel out of the land of Egypt,' but—'As Jehovah liveth, which brought up and led the seed of the house of Israel out of the land of the north.'[7] Between past and present, there were points of contrast, also, as of resemblance. Israel was not leaving Babylon

---

[1] Isa. lii. 12.
[2] Ezek. xx. 34.
[3] Isa. xi. 15; xliii. 16.
[4] Micah vii. 15.
[5] Isa. xi. 16.
[6] Isa. xlviii. 21; xxxv. 6.
[7] Jer. xxiii. 7, 8.

by stealth, a fugitive, as it had left Egypt in the days of old.[1] No Pharaoh thundered in pursuit. But, on the other hand, no Moses went at the head of the people.

These glowing words and images of their prophets, which assured them of the divine protection and promised a glorious issue to their enterprise, brought the exiles forth from Babylon with every sign of hopefulness and rejoicing. The departure from the city was a national festival, shared in both by those who went and those who stayed behind. Glad music sounded, and the pilgrims were accompanied beyond the walls by friendly crowds, dancing mirthfully to the strains of flute and tabret.[2] The bands of choristers and minstrels chanted the songs of deliverance. The Levites and chosen men[3] passed in front of the long procession, carrying on high the vessels of the Temple. In the midst of his people rode the Prince of the House of David, on whom rested so many

---

[1] 'Ye shall not go out in haste, neither shall ye go by flight.'—Isa. lii. 12.

[2] Apoc. Ezra v. 2, 3.

[3] 'Be ye clean, ye that bear the vessels of Jehovah.'—Isa. lii. 11.

secret hopes. It was a moment of exaltation, in which the dangers and toils of the morrow and of many days and years to come were forgotten, and nothing was thought of but the great fact that now the Captivity was over and Israel freed. They hasted to be gone. It was as though they heard a voice from Jerusalem, calling her children home.[1] The cry sounded in their ears — 'Away! away! Pass ye, pass ye through the gates; clear ye the way of the people!'[2] A great Prophet, an onlooker in the spirit two centuries before, has drawn the picture of that strangely stirring scene. The noise was great by reason of the multitude of men. They have broken up; they have passed on to the gate; they have gone out. Their King is passed on before them, and Jehovah is at their head.[3]

---

[1] Isa. lii. 8, 9. [2] Ibid. 11, lxii. 10. [3] Micah ii. 12, 13.

CHAPTER V.

Among the Ruins.

THE homeward journey of the exiles is passed over without comment in Jewish annals. It was long and tedious, but apparently uneventful. Following the caravan route by Thapsacus, Tadmor, and Damascus, they had a distance of over eight hundred miles to travel, most of them on foot—a toilsome pilgrimage which was not completed until the fourth or fifth month after the departure from Babylon.

The day so long and ardently desired had come at last. The Bene ha-Golah had entered on their heritage. They breathed the air of freedom, they trod on soil that was their own, they found themselves among scenes familiar to all of them by tradition, and bound up with many pious and patriotic memories. There was a natural outburst of joy and gratitude; then, the darker side of things presented itself, and many illusions were dispelled. If the Children of the Exile had counted on regaining the former kingdom of Judah, they were soon undeceived. The Chaldæan conquest had left Judea a kind of no man's land, virtually emptied of its population and open to all comers. The Arab tribesmen had roamed unchecked over its deserted fields. The Samaritans from the north, the Edomites from the south, had pushed beyond their borders, and established themselves almost within sight of Jerusalem. These intruders had to be dispossessed, before the newcomers could occupy even the merest strip of territory. Probably the command of Cyrus sufficed for this without any use of force. The governor of Abar-Nahara,[1] the Trans-Euphratene, had his instructions, and took measures by which a sufficient space was cleared for the colonists. Jerusalem was restored to them, with the towns and villages in its immediate neighbourhood,[2] such as Bethle-

---

[1] Ezra iv. 11.
[2] Of the places mentioned in Ezra ii. 20-35, scarcely one lies at a distance of more than twenty miles from Jerusalem.

hem, Anathoth, the birthplace of Jeremiah, Nob, the ancient priestly town. North-east, towards Jordan, they had Jericho, and to the north, Gibeon and Bethel. Not until a later date did the new community reach southward in the Negeb as far as Hebron, and westward, towards the coast, as far as Lydda. The whole extent of territory originally repossessed by them, lying chiefly to the north of Jerusalem, measured no more than twenty-five miles in length and twenty miles in breadth. Even this contracted area they had not exclusively to themselves. The Edomites [1] and Samaritans, not daring to resist the royal command, had sullenly withdrawn from the lands and villages they had seized, and made way for the ancient owners of the soil. But it was not possible to oust completely, at least from the country districts, the foreigners and Jewish half-breeds who had squatted

---

[1] It is noteworthy that the Edomites are not once named in the Books of Ezra and Nehemiah among the enemies of the Jewish colony. Apparently the power of Edom had suffered from the fall of the Chaldæan empire, with which it was allied at the time of the destruction of Jerusalem. (Obad. 10-14; Ezek. xxxv. 5; Ps. cxxxvii. 7.) Only at a date long after the Return did Edom (though always a troublesome neighbour—see *infra*, p. 230) again become formidable to the Judeans.

there in considerable numbers, and the presence of this pagan element in the midst of it must have added largely to the early troubles of the colony.

Still more disheartening was the condition in which the exiles found the land on their return. To them, as to their fathers, it was 'the land of promise,' but no longer could it be called a 'goodly land,' 'flowing with milk and honey.' The devastation wrought by the Chaldæan armies in the last years of the monarchy, followed by more than a half-century of neglect, had made parts of the once fertile country little better than a wilderness. Forests had been cut down,[1] fields had gone out of cultivation, and hill-slopes once clothed with vineyards and olive groves were now bare even of soil.[2] The writings of the prophets teem with allusions to the miserable state of Judea during the Captivity. It was a 'broken-down land,' a 'land turned upside down;' more inhospitable than the desert;

---

[1] Jer. vi. 6.
[2] On the terrace-cultivation of Judea, and the need of constant care and labour to maintain it, see Kitto, *Physical Geography of the Holy Land*, 32; Stanley, *Sinai and Palestine*, 120.

blighted as if by a curse.¹ The prophetic picture may be overcharged, since the country had never been wholly depopulated. But the reality was bad enough, and the aspect of those barren hillsides and wasted fields could not but have a depressing effect on men who had newly come from the most fruitful region of the world. At Jerusalem, the goal of their wanderings, the saddest sight of all awaited them. For fifty years the Holy City had lain as the destroyer had left it, tenantless, dark and silent—no light of lamp seen, no footfall, no sound of millstones heard.² On 'the mountain of the House' the trees were growing wild, and the jackals prowled among heaps of shattered masonry.³ Great piles of crumbling stonework and charred timbers marked the sites of palaces and towers. The wreck of the Temple buildings littered and choked the streets;⁴ the city walls and gates were levelled with the ground. It was no wonder if the 'spirit of heaviness' fell upon the Bene

---

[1] Isa. xlix. 19; xxiv. 1, 6; Ezek. vi. 14; Jer. iv. 26; ix. 11; viii. 13.
[2] Jer. xxv. 10; xxxiii. 10.
[3] Jer. xxvi. 18; ix. 10, 11.
[4] Lam. iv. 1.

ha-Golah, as they stood among the ruins of Jerusalem, and thought of its departed beauty and of past glories buried under its dust and stones.

But the needs of the moment were pressing, the courage of the people and their leaders mounted with their difficulties, and they set themselves resolutely to the task of bringing some measure of order from out the confusion around them. The chiefs of the community and the families which belonged to Jerusalem by their origin remained in the city; the rest dispersed, seeking the abodes of their fathers. The Roll of the Congregation was the Domesday Book which regulated the division of the land and the succession to property, but room had everywhere to be found for those whose patrimony lay beyond the narrow confines of the new Judea. There were of necessity many hardships and privations to be endured by the settlers before they succeeded in making for themselves even the semblance of a home. The rudest work of all fell to the inhabitants of Jerusalem. There, before even the humblest dwelling could be erected, the ground had to be laboriously cleared of the rubbish that encumbered it; and for months the Prince and the nobles of Judah, who had dwelt in stately mansions at Babylon, had to content themselves with the shelter of huts or tents, set up on the sites of the ruined palaces of their ancestors.

In view of their difficulties at the outset, the necessity of finding the bare means of subsistence, it might have been pardoned to the exiles had they postponed for a time the attempt to restore the national worship. But nothing was further from their thoughts. The tide of religious enthusiasm still ran strong; they were impatient to make a beginning of the most important of all their duties. In this they were guided by a sound instinct. Not only the priesthood, which was influential in proportion to its numbers, but the whole community felt that they had really no claim to exist until the Temple was raised again, or at least until the sacrifices were resumed. Scarcely had they set their hands to the work of building their houses and tilling their fields, when the first day of the seventh month brought them 'as one man'[1] to Jerusalem. This was

---

[1] Ezra iii. 1.

the month Tisri, the festival-month of the Jewish Calendar, in which fell the Feast of Trumpets, the Day of Atonement, the Feast of Tabernacles. Already, it would seem, the colonists had begun to take alarm at the attitude of the Amme ha-Aretz, the heathen populations which surrounded them on every side. Fearing either an attempt to hinder them in their sacred task, or perhaps a scarcely less unwelcome offer of assistance such as was afterwards actually made, they hurried on the erection of the altar of burnt-offering, setting it up on its ancient foundations, which had been discovered beneath the debris that strewed the Temple hill. The first of Tisri (September) of the year 537 became an interesting date in Jewish history. On that day, in view of the gathered thousands of Israel, the priests and Levites once more did their office on Jewish soil, the blood of the victims flowed, and the smoke of the holocaust rose from Mount Zion. Fifty years had passed since the ceasing of the daily oblation, which was now offered each morning and evening as of yore.

The simple altar,[1] hastily erected among the

---

[1] This altar is described by Hecatæus of Abdera (circ. 300

ruins of Jerusalem, was a pledge to the people of divine favour and protection. At the same time, it reminded them that the work of restoration was but begun. Wanting the Temple, they could worship with maimed rites only. Wanting the Holy of Holies, into which it was his to enter on the great Day of Atonement, the High Priest was High Priest only in name. No time was lost in setting about the necessary preparations for building. They had the promise of help from Cyrus, but in the meantime money was needed, and needed at once. Zerubbabel, as civil head of the community, and probably its wealthiest member, set the example of liberality. He presented to the Temple treasury 1000 golden pieces,[1] 500 pounds of silver, a number of priestly robes and of sacrificial vessels.[2] The chiefs of the people, the 'heads of houses,' made a dona-

B.C.) as 'a square altar, not of hewn but of unhewn stones gathered together.'—Josephus, *Contra Apion.* i. 22.

[1] The *darkemonim* of Neh. vii. 70, Ezra ii. 69, probably = *darics*, and is so rendered in the Revised Version. The Authorised Version has *drams* (= *drachmæ*). The daric, the ordinary Persian gold coin (Greek *dareikos*), though current in Palestine in the days of the Chronicler, did not exist at the time of the Return. Its value was about that of the English guinea.

[2] Neh. vii. 70, from which the words 'pounds of silver'

tion of 20,000 golden pieces and 2,000 pounds of silver. An equal sum was contributed by the common people, with, in addition, an offering of priestly robes. Two things appear from the narrative of this national subscription—the poverty of the priesthood, and the generosity and religious zeal of the laity. The building fund thus raised was modest indeed when compared with the vast accumulations of treasure which preceded the erection of the first Temple. But it represented, in the circumstances of the time, a spirit of self-denial, a deep, personal interest in the undertaking shared by all ranks of the community, which scarcely appear in the brilliant days of David and Solomon.

The preparations made for the building of the second Temple were at various points curiously similar to those made for the building of the first, five hundred years before. As in the days of Solomon, cedar-wood was obtained from Lebanon by contract with the Phœnicians, who—again as in those days—

---

have evidently dropped out after the numeral 500.—Bertheau-Ryssel, 30: Schultz, in Lange's *Bibelwerk*, *ad loc.*

were paid, not in money, but in the produce of the land, corn, wine and oil.[1] The colonists had not yet had time to reap a harvest; to meet these costs, they must mortgage the harvests of the future. King Solomon had employed his own subjects, in squads of 10,000 at a time, in felling the trees of the Lebanon forests. This part of the work, on a much smaller scale, was now done by the Sidonian and Tyrian lumbermen, who—exactly as in Solomon's day—floated the precious timber along the coast to Joppa, where the rafts were broken up, and whence the logs were conveyed by the Jews with no little toil over the forty miles of rough road to Jerusalem. The skilled labour which Solomon had at command was almost exclusively Phœnician. But the Jews, during the Babylonian captivity, had made progress in the arts of masonry and carpentry, and did not need to hire foreign craftsmen. The wages of the artisans were paid in money from the Temple fund. The ruins of Jerusalem were the quarry from which they drew a large part of their materials, and many of the

---

[1] Ezra iii. 7; *cp.* 1 Kings v. 11; 2 Chron. ii. 10-16.

enormous bevel-edged blocks, hewn and dressed by King Hiram's masons centuries ago, were doubtless found available for the construction of the second Temple.

The means at the disposal of the builders did not admit of rapid progress being made. Labour was necessarily scarce: King Solomon's army of workmen far outnumbered the entire population of the new Judea.[1] The clearing of the site, which lay buried under ponderous masses of ruin, put a sufficient strain on their resources, and six months had passed before this was done, and material for building got together. The laying of the foundation-stone was made the occasion of a religious ceremony, arranged as far as possible on the lines of the stately functions of the past. On a day in the second month of the second year of the Return—the month Ijar (April) 536—the Bene ha-Golah once more assembled at Jerusalem. Crowds of people blackened the Temple hill. The priests, resplendent in their new apparel, the Levites, choristers and musicians, were marshalled to their places in the centre of the throng. The

---

[1] 1 Kings v. 15, 16.

priests blew their silver trumpets, the Levites clashed their cymbals, the singers of the clan of Asaph raised the hymn of praise. Choir answered choir, filling the air with strains of joy.

'O give thanks unto Jehovah, for He is good!'

—and another set of voices sent back the glad refrain :—

> '*For His mercy endureth for ever!—*
>
> *He remembered us in our low estate.*
> *For His mercy endureth for ever!*
> *He hath delivered us from our enemies.*
> *For His mercy endureth for ever!*[1]—'

Then Zerubbabel came forward. As Prince of Judah, head of the kingly house whose founders had raised the first Temple, it was his part and privilege to lay the foundation of the second.[2] A great shout burst from the assembled multitude as they saw this ceremony performed and the corner-stone set in its place—then, as the echoes rolled away, another sound was heard, of ominous meaning. There were many aged men among the priests and chiefs of the people, some among the spectators, whose eyes had seen the glory of the former House, and

---

[1] Ezra iii. 11. *Cp.* 1 Chron. xvi. 34; Ps. cxxxvi.
[2] Zech. iv. 9.

had seen it desecrated and spoiled by the heathen, devoured by the flames. The rush of memories brought up by the events of the day overcame these survivors of a past generation. They realised too well that with the Temple of their youth a nation had fallen, and that only a colony or a sect could gather round its successor. They felt too keenly the hopelessness of expecting that the new sanctuary, the meagre preparations for which they saw before them, could ever rival the beauty and magnificence of the old. The young generation might rejoice, but for them the days of their 'mourning for Zion' would never end. The loud wailing of these ancients of Israel mingled audibly with the jubilant outcry; next moment it was drowned in the clash of cymbals, and the mighty shout which the people, on hearing it, raised with redoubled vigour. But the note of sadness had been struck, and its vibration never died away. Henceforth there was no festivity for Israel without its undertone of melancholy, no joy of achievement without its tinge of regret.

CHAPTER VI.

Jew and Samaritan.

FOR some time the work thus inaugurated went on briskly. The Levites, according to ancient precedent,[1] were appointed as overseers; an excellent spirit prevailed among them — they addressed themselves to the task, says the Chronicler, 'as one man.'[2] But scarcely had the walls begun to rise when a difficulty presented itself, and the colonists were once more, as at the time of the building of the altar, unpleasantly reminded of the interest taken in their proceedings by the peoples of the land. The ceremony of the month Ijar had, it is said, attracted to the neighbourhood of Jerusalem a concourse of the aliens, who listened with wonder to the blare of trumpets and the joyous tumult amid which the foundation-stone was laid.[3] At all events,

---

[1] Ezra iii. 8; cp. Numbers iv. 2, 3; 1 Chron. xxiii. 24.
[2] Ezra iii. 9.   [3] Apoc. Ezra v. 66, 67; cp. Ezra iii. 13.

the report that the Jews had begun to build their Temple spread quickly, and caused a certain degree of excitement among the non-Jewish populations.

The Chronicler gives no name to these Amme ha-Aretz, describing them simply as 'the adversaries of Judah and Benjamin.'[1] But the narrative itself fixes their identity. They were the strange people, or rather congeries of peoples, known afterwards to the Jews by the generic and contemptuous name of *Kuthim*[2] —the Samaritans of the New Testament. The account given by the Jewish writer[3] of the origin of this people and their first settlement in Palestine, though coloured by later prejudice, may be taken as fairly historical. As a result of the Assyrian system of deportation —by which, in order to punish or prevent revolt, countries and provinces remote from each other were forced to interchange their inhabitants — there had been settled in the northern part of Palestine perhaps the most extraordinary jumble of nationalities known to

---

[1] Ezra iv. 1.
[2] *i.e.*, 'people of Kutha,' a city of Babylonia.
[3] In 2 Kings xvii. 24 ff.

history. There were Chaldæans from Babylon and Kutha, Syrians from Hamath, Elamites from Susa: even, it would seem, Phœnicians from Sidon[1] and Arabs from Petra.[2] These peoples had been planted in the land at different times, by three successive monarchs of Assyria—by Sargon, by Esar-haddon, and lastly, by Assur-bani-pal.[3] At the date of the Jewish return from Babylon, Sargon's colonists had inhabited Samaria for about 180 years, Assur-bani-pal's for about 130 years. During that period, under stress of circumstances, there had formed itself out of these heterogeneous elements something resembling a people, capable of common sentiment and action. In this evolution the native Israelitish population had unquestionably played a very important part. The Assyrian conquests and deportations, ruthless and sweeping as they were, had still left a great number of Israelites in the land, for, as has been said,

---

[1] Josephus, *Ant.* xii. 5, sect. 5.
[2] Schrader, *Die Keilinschriften u. d. Alt. Test.* ii. 276.
[3] The unnamed king of 2 Kings xvii. 24 is Sargon; see Rawlinson, *Ancient Monarchies*, ii. 410. The name 'Asnapper' in Ezra iv. 10 is almost certainly a corruption of 'Assur-banipal' (Sardanapalus).—Schrader, *Keilinschriften*, ii. 376.

'a country, and particularly a mountainous country, cannot be drained of its inhabitants like a fish-pond.' To some extent, these relics of the northern kingdom held together, and preserved their distinction of race and religion.[1] But the mass of them lived with, intermarried with the heathen colonists, and, without weaning them from their idolatries—which, indeed, owing to the corruption of religious life in the northern kingdom, they were little fitted to do—taught them something of the knowledge and worship of Jehovah. These facts are presented by the Jewish historian in a more or less legendary form. The foreign colonists, newly settled in the land, suffer from the ravages of wild beasts, and at once conclude that the local divinity has taken offence at their neglect of his shrine. They petition the king of Assyria to send back from Nineveh a priest of Israel, who shall 'teach them the

---

[1] See 2 Chron. xxx. 11; xxxiv. 9. The 'Galilee' of the Books of Maccabees (cp. 1st Maccab. v. 14) and of the N.T. is a region populated, at least to some extent, by Israelites of the ancient northern kingdom, who had escaped deportation, and kept themselves distinct from the Kuthim.—Bertheau, *Abhänd-lungen zur Gesch. Israels*, 360.

manner of the god of the land.'[1] The king complies, and sends them a priest who re-establishes at Bethel the ancient cult of the calf. This they call the worship of Jehovah; but along with this they carry on their native idolatries, the men of each city or province setting up their god in one of the 'high places' of Samaria. The reforming zeal of King Josiah carries him beyond his frontier; he heads a crusade into Samaria, destroys the 'high places,' and massacres the priests.[2] But the Samaritans remain unconverted. A debased form of Jehovah-worship continues to flourish among them, alongside the pagan cults imported from their earlier homes. 'So these nations feared Jehovah, and served their graven images; their children likewise, and their children's children, as did their fathers, so do they unto this day'[3]—such is the religious history of the Kuthim, from the Jewish orthodox point of view, which probably in the main was not unjust.

Not long after the laying of the corner-stone, a deputation from this people arrived

---

[1] 2 Kings xvii. 27. [2] *Ibid.*, xxiii. 15-20. [3] *Ibid.*, xvii. 41.

at Jerusalem, with the request that they might be allowed to take part in the building of the Temple. Their claim to this honour, according to the statement of the Chronicler, was based solely on the ground that they were co-religionists: 'Let us build with you; for we serve your God, as ye do; and we do sacrifice unto Him since the days of Esarhaddon, king of Assyria, which brought us up hither.'[1] Possibly, in making their offer, they may have put forward a claim to affinity of race as well as of religion, which the Chronicler passes over in silence. What they proposed was virtually a federation of North and South, with Jerusalem as its ecclesiastical centre. The proposal was evidently made in perfect good faith; the Samaritans are introduced into Jewish history as 'the adversaries,' but that is by anticipation; their first appearance on the scene was quite amicable. They had apparently grown weary of the multiform idolatries which distracted and disunited them, and hindered their national development. They had a sincere if not very enlightened

---

[1] Ezra iv. 2.

appreciation of the higher worship of the Jews. And they were naturally drawn towards Jerusalem by the influence of the Israelites who had mingled with them or who lived among them, and who had long since forgotten the ancient grudge against Judah. There is no statement of the terms they offered, but these, if they were to have any chance of acceptance, must have included the promise of conformity to Jewish ritual and doctrine, as established at Jerusalem.

These overtures of the Samaritans at once opened the question—the burning question of the time, which the community had to face again and again—as to what should be the attitude of the Jewish people towards its heathen neighbours. The question came up early in the history of the colony; sooner or later, from the nature of the case, it was bound to rise. There was now no physical frontier between Judaism and heathenism. All they possessed of the land of their fathers was a few square miles, vaguely delimited; the Gentiles surrounded them on every side, pressed in upon them, would not leave them to themselves. This close contiguity of the

Amme ha-Aretz, their interference in Jewish affairs, was a perpetual grievance with the colony. The nations 'compassed them about' —buzzed round them and annoyed them like a swarm of bees.[1] Contact with the heathen was unavoidable. In this respect, they were little better off now than they had been in Babylon. 'Woe is me,' a poet of the day complains, 'that I sojourn in Meshech, that I dwell among the tents of Kedar!'[2]

There were two ways of looking at and dealing with this Gentile question; consequently, two parties rose among the Jews themselves— one, progressist, the other, retrograde. The great Prophet of the Exile had put in the forefront of his teaching the mission of Israel to the Gentiles; he had again and again vindicated the right of the Gentiles to the privileges enjoyed by the Jews; in one of the most daring flights of prophecy, he had thrown open to the Gentiles the door of the Levitical priesthood.[3] There were men of his school, imbued with his ideas, among the Bene ha-Golah—prophets themselves, or partisans of prophecy. It was a cherished belief of the people that the Mes-

---
[1] Ps. cxviii. 11, 12.   [2] Ps. cxx. 5.   [3] Isa. lxvi. 21.

sianic time drew near. But one grand feature
of that Messianic time was to be an ingathering
of the Gentiles, a flowing of all peoples and
tongues to the holy mountain, a rending of the
veil spread over the nations.[1] Had it not been
written that strangers should build the walls
of Zion?[2] What was the duty of Israel,
restored by a marvellous providence to its
native soil? To expand or concentrate? To
take the offered hand of the Gentiles, or to
thrust it scornfully aside?

Against this progressist, this prophetic party,
was the great mass of the people. Theirs
was a different ideal. They had no taste for
the altruism of the Prophets. To preserve a
separate national existence was the sum of
their hopes. It had been impressed upon them
during the Captivity that the first duty and
highest merit of the true Israelite was isolation
from the heathen, and they had not forgotten
the lesson. Jehovah was their God, and they,
and no others, should build His temple. The
Samaritans, say what they might, were idolaters,
and hatred of idolatry was now a passion with
the Jews. The Samaritans were a mongrel

---

[1] Isa. lvi. 8; xxv. 6, 7.   [2] Isa. lx. 10.

race, whose claim to kinship was an insult. They would have no dealings with the Samaritans.

Zerubbabel and the chiefs of the community whom he called into council were able to judge and settle the question on grounds of policy. The offer made them was in some respects tempting. It was flattering to Jewish pride to have Samaria thus coming as suitor to Jerusalem; there might seem a prospect of restoring something like the state of things that had existed before the breaking off of the northern kingdom. By this time it had become obvious that the work of rearing the Temple must tax severely, if it did not overtax, the strength and resources of the little colony; the Samaritans were numerous, and able to bring needed hands and treasure to the building. To refuse this offer was to make enemies of people who were willing to be friends. On the other hand, the Jewish leaders had to consider that the zeal of their own people, still in its first fervour, would certainly be abated, and their pride and pleasure in the Temple materially lessened, if this half-heathen race were called in to labour by their side. There was further the probability that the Samaritans, if their present demand were conceded, might seek to draw the bond of union closer still. In the Jewish economy Church and State were practically identified; to give these outsiders a voice in the one was to invite their interference with the other. Thus all the precautions taken to secure the purity of the Jewish race would be made ineffective, and the colony, numerically weak, might in the end be overborne, swamped by this influx of alien elements. They were prepared to receive, they had already received, proselytes from the Gentiles. They would welcome all those of their own people, whether belonging to the North or to the South, who forsook their idolatries, severed themselves from the heathen, and owned the spiritual supremacy of Jerusalem. But the Samaritans were neither Jews nor Gentiles; they were an amalgam, and all the more dangerous on that account. Zerubbabel and his colleagues debated and decided the question without reference either to the prophetic ideal or the popular prejudice. Their reply was diplomatic, but firm. They fell back on their charter, the Edict of Cyrus, which authorised them to build their own Temple, but not to enter into engagements with any neighbouring people for that purpose. 'It is not for you and for us to build a House to our God; since we, and we only, build for Jehovah the God of Israel, as Cyrus the King hath given us command.'[1]

The Jews, having thus shaken off these would-be allies, took up the work of building with renewed ardour. Mortally offended at their rebuff, the envoys left Jerusalem; the Samaritan schism, with all its evil consequences, had begun. Soon the colony was made to feel what powers of injury its neighbours possessed. The contest between the two peoples was transferred to the court of Babylon. The Samaritans had their paid agents at court, working by bribery and other means against the Jews. What form their charges and insinuations took is not stated, but can easily be guessed at. The Jews were disloyal subjects of the Great King. Their anxiety for the building of their temple was a mere blind, under cover of which they were fortifying Mount Moriah. They were conspiring to regain their independence, and to seat their

[1] Ezra iv. 3.

Pekhah on the throne of his ancestors.—The Samaritans were perfectly unscrupulous in their opposition. They were ready to claim kinship with the Jews or to disclaim it as it suited them, and at the court of Babylon they put their Babylonian and Elamite origin to the front. They had the means of bribery in abundance. And as they were a considerable people, holding the fortified places of Samaria, and in a position to be useful in certain eventualities, their representations had naturally more weight with the imperial counsellors than those of the Jews, who from the military point of view were of little or no account. The Jews placed their dependence on the royal favour and the royal decree. But Cyrus had the affairs of an immense empire, of which he was the founder, to think of; he must of necessity leave the details of administration to others; and—from any point of view save one which the king and his ministers were incapable of taking—the wellbeing of the Jewish colony was the veriest of details. Cyrus was a soldier, and the greater part of his life was spent in the camp, not in the palace. Amid the rush and turmoil of his warlike career, in which intervals of peace were rare, he either forgot his Jewish subjects or handed over the charge of them to others.[1] There was no revocation of the Edict, but its purpose might be frustrated indirectly. Those subsidies which the king had promised, on which the Jews had counted, might be quietly intercepted. Inquiries might be made, answers demanded, and thus the work delayed. And if it still went on in spite of these obstacles, the Samaritans, secure of support in high quarters, might make a show of actual violence, and force the builders to desist in fear of their lives.[2] The chiefs of the colony exerted themselves to overcome this opposition, but without success. The 'deceitful tongue'[3] prevailed, and the Jewish officials at court, whose influence with the king had formerly been considerable, were now reduced to despair.[4]

This deadlock in Jewish affairs, due in the first instance to the ill-will of the Samaritans, lasted for years—years which are left completely blank in the annals of the nation. The effort to carry out the great purpose of

---

[1] Josephus *Ant.* xi. 2, sect. 1.
[2] Ezra iv. 4, where for 'troubled' read 'frightened.'
[3] Ps. cxx. 2.   [4] Dan. x. 2.

the Return was not at once abandoned; but as each renewed attempt was met by renewed threats and hindrances, the people grew discouraged, their zeal flagged and their hopes fell. The allusions of the prophets who stood forward at a later day convey the impression that Zerubbabel and Joshua and the other leading men at Jerusalem scarcely rose to the height of their opportunities, and resigned themselves somewhat too easily to inaction. There is a tacit rebuke in the words of a contemporary Psalmist:—' It is better to trust in Jehovah than to put confidence in princes.'[1] The Jewish leaders had been disposed to rely too much on the promises of Cyrus, and too little on themselves. It became a kind of standing excuse with them that 'the time was not come, the time for building the house of Jehovah'[2]—they were watching the political horizon, trying to make interest at court, when the simpler and bolder course of going on with the work at all hazards, in terms of their charter, might have solved the difficulty. But in truth these intrigues of the Samaritans

---

[1] Ps. cxviii. 9. [2] Hagg. i. 2.

were only one among many things which quenched the enthusiasm of the people, and killed the sanguine spirit of the early days. The Bene ha-Golah had come back from Babylon fully persuaded that the Messianic time was near, expecting to reap without delay the reward of their self-sacrifice, and to see the opening of that golden age of Israel which the great Prophet had so gloriously pictured. They had looked for a birth of the nation without travail.[1] They had counted on regaining their land to its uttermost border, and beyond.[2] They had dreamt of a day when once again at Jerusalem silver should be as stones and cedars as sycamores;[3] when all nations should bow humbly at the feet of Israel, their riches pour in as a stream, and their kings be foster-fathers of Jehovah's people.[4] With whatever reluctance, these hopes had to be owned as premature and given up in face of the grim reality. The rapturous joy of the Return, which had seemed like a dream, passed like a dream; the visionaries had to come down to the lower

---

[1] Isa. lxvi. 7.
[2] Isa. xxvi. 15.
[3] 1 Kings x. 27; cp. Isa. lx. 17.
[4] *Ibid.*, xi. 14; xlix. 23.

level of actual experience, and adjust themselves to conditions of life which were by comparison tame and sordid. They found themselves in possession of a mere shred of the land which was rightfully theirs, poor and defenceless, harassed on all sides by the heathen, neglected by their royal patron. The Prophet's words were true in a wider sense than he intended—'they had looked for much, and lo, it had come to little.'[1] Even their countrymen in Babylon seemed to have forgotten them; neither in men nor in money did they send that help which the struggling colony so urgently needed, and which it had a right to expect.[2] The feeling of disappointment and discontent grew and spread, and the chiefs of the community, no longer spurred on by popular sentiment, became less energetic in combating their opponents, more inclined to sit down with folded hands under defeat. The year 532, the sixth year of the Return, was marked by an event distinctly adverse to

---

[1] Hagg. i. 9.
[2] According to Jewish tradition, Cyrus, taking alarm at the drain on the population of Babylonia, forbade further emigration. That so much is made of the episode of the Crowns (Zech. vi. 10) shows it to have been exceptional.

Jewish interests. In that year Cyrus made over the monarchy of Babylon to his elder son Cambyses, who cared nothing for the Jews, and whose character forbade any hope of obtaining indulgent treatment from him. The zeal which had built the altar, founded the Temple, and repulsed the Samaritans, had by this time cooled down. The people began to think more of their material than of their religious needs. The ruin-heaps on Moriah, the vacant site, ceased either to inspire or reproach them; they accepted the situation, and were now mainly concerned to make it as tolerable as possible for themselves. The rich built them fine houses in Jerusalem, wainscoted with costly timber,[1] mimicking the luxury they had known at Babylon. The poor were no better in this respect than the rich; every man looked after his own interests, without a thought for anything save house and fields.[2] Yet with all this the colony did not prosper. The times grew worse instead of mending. Bad seasons came;

---

[1] Hagg. i. 4. Grätz suggests, with the timber procured for the Temple—*Gesch.* ii. 88.
[2] Hagg. i. 9.

drought, hailstorms, mildew spoiled the harvests; the fruit of vine and fig-tree, of olive and pomegranate, failed, so that there was dearth in the land, distress among the people.[1] The last hope of Jewish patriotism was extinguished by the death of Cyrus in the year 529, the ninth year of the Return. In a 'battle of kites and crows,' fought on the trackless steppes against the savage tribes of the north, the great king fell. The career of Cyrus ends obscurely, as it had begun. His body is said to have been carried from the shore of the Caspian to Pasargadæ, and buried there in a splendid mausoleum with honours almost divine. The inscription on his tomb, as recorded by the Greeks, shows at least the estimation in which this prince was held by antiquity.—*O man, whosoever thou art, and whencesoever thou comest—for come I know thou wilt—I am Cyrus, the Founder of the Persian Empire. Envy me not the little earth that covers my body.*[2] The real epitaph was simpler:—*I am Cyrus, the King, the*

---

[1] Hagg. i. 6, 10, 11; ii. 16, 17.
[2] Plutarch, *Life of Alexander*.

Achæmenian.[1] Though Cyrus had not done for the Jews all that had been expected, their obligation to him was never forgotten. As the man who released them from captivity and authorised the building of the Temple, he holds a unique place in Jewish history and tradition. Of all monarchs of the Gentiles, says the quaint legend in the Second Targum of Esther, it was given to Cyrus alone to take his seat on the throne of Solomon.[2]

Under Cambyses, who now succeeded to the throne of empire, the condition of the Jewish colonists became doubly wretched. This prince appears on the vivid page of

---

[1] Lenormant, *Ancient Hist.*, ii. 93.

[2] According to the legend, this throne was the masterwork of the wisdom of Solomon. It was made of ivory, overlaid with gold, encrusted with gems, and guarded by golden figures of lions and eagles. 'After the conquest of Jerusalem, King Nebuchadnezzar desired to seat himself on this throne; but as he set his foot on the first step, one of the golden lions stretched out its right paw, and struck him on the left foot, so that he went lame to his dying day. Alexander of Macedon brought the throne of Solomon to Egypt; and when Shishak, king of Egypt, in like manner essayed to take his seat thereon, the same fate befel him as had befallen Nebuchadnezzar, and he received the name of "the limping Pharaoh" all his days. . . . Only to Cyrus the Persian was it vouchsafed to sit on the throne of Solomon, because this he had merited by his concern for the building of the Temple.'—See *Bibliotheca Rabbinica: Midrasch Esther*, 79.

Herodotus as a furious madman, scarcely less formidable to his friends than to his enemies. The chronic insanity[1] may be doubted, but it is certain that this son of Cyrus was a man of violent passions, a slave to his caprices, and capable of cruelties which were not unnaturally set down as proofs of a disordered mind. Plato says of him that he had been 'badly brought up;' Herodotus, that he was epileptic; Josephus, that he was 'by nature wicked.' He seems to have been a ruler of the type of Ivan the Terrible—a man of ungovernable impulse, armed with unlimited power. The great object of Cambyses was the conquest of Egypt—an object which could not be carried out without directly affecting the Judæans, who lay in the track of an advance from Asia into Africa. An immense army was got together; treaties were made with the Phœnicians and Idumeans —the former to help by sea, the latter to conduct the Persian host over the waterless desert between Palestine and Egypt. Before setting out on this expedition,[2] Cambyses

---

[1] Herod. iii. 30. [2] Duncker, Gesch. des Altertums, iv. 443.

secretly put to death his brother Bardes, apparently to prevent any attempt at usurpation in his absence—a crime which afterwards cost him dear. In the year 527 he invaded Egypt, overthrew Pharaoh in a pitched battle at Pelusium, captured Memphis, and made himself master of the land of the Nile.

Scarcely any worse calamity could befall a land than the passing through it of one of those vast unwieldy armies, or rather hordes, which the Persian kings led in war. Drawn from all countries and provinces of the far-stretching empire, without order or discipline, attended by countless swarms of camp-followers,[1] moving leisurely onwards, and straggling widely out on either side of the line of march, they spread ruin around and left desolation behind them. The campaign of Cambyses pressed with special severity upon Palestine. The strip of land between the Syrian Desert and the Mediterranean was almost too narrow to serve as a highway

---

[1] Herodotus refers to the camp-followers of the Persian armies as outnumbering the fighting men; and describes those armies as drinking up the rivers and eating up the lands in their passage (viii. 186, 187).

for the hosts of Asia pouring down upon Egypt; scarcely any part of it could escape being trodden under foot. Cambyses, after completing his conquest, was in no hurry to leave it; he lingered in Egypt year after year, and during this time there was probably a military occupation of Palestine, to secure the passage of reinforcements or the line of retreat. The Jewish colonists, in addition to their other hardships, had now to make acquaintance with some, at least, of the miseries of war. Their sufferings during those dark years were long remembered: Cambyses figures in their traditions as 'the second Nebuchadnezzar.' The Idumeans and Phœnicians, possibly the Samaritans also, were on the best of terms with Cambyses; these peoples were able to assist him in his enterprise. The Jews were too weak to be used, too insignificant to be noticed, and now they lay at the mercy of their old enemies, who might work their will on them with impunity. There was no peace in the land because of the oppressor; no hire for man or beast, but only military requisitions; no keeping of one's property safe from marauders—to lay by money was simply to 'put it into a bag with holes.'¹ In those days the fortunes of the colony touched their lowest ebb.

During his first years in Egypt, Cambyses pursued the same line of policy by which his father had conciliated the Babylonians; he declared himself a worshipper of the gods of Egypt, made splendid gifts to the priests, was initiated at Saïs into the mysteries of Neit, and took the native title of *Mesut-Ra*, 'Offspring of the Sun.'² But after the disastrous failure of his campaign against the Ethiopians his treatment of the Egyptians changed. Returning from that expedition, in which two armies had been sacrificed, he found great rejoicing in the land of Egypt—an Apis had been born, the divine bull, the incarnation of Phtah, supreme god of Memphis. Cambyses, imagining that the priests and people were exulting over his reverses, and carried away by a sudden gust of fury, drew his sword and mortally wounded the sacred bull-calf³

¹ Zech. viii. 10 ; Hagg. i. 6.
² Lenormant, *Ancient Hist.*, ii. 97.   *Records of the Past*, x. 49 ff.
³ The statement of Herodotus as to the killing of Apis is contested by Brugsch (*Gesch. Ægyptens*, 745 ff.) The discovery of the Apis-stele, however, does not disprove the story.

—an outrage which lost him the loyalty of the Egyptians, who ever after held his name in abhorrence. And now troubles crowded thick upon Cambyses. A revolution broke out at the seat of empire from which he had been so long absent,[1] headed by the Magian Gaumâta, who took the name of the murdered Bardes, and proclaimed himself king. 'The lie grew in the provinces,' says the Behistun Inscription significantly. Cambyses left Egypt in frenzied haste, and was on his way homeward to chastise the impostor and restore his authority, when, at an obscure town in Syria, he put an end to his life. The Greeks saw in this tragic event the remorse of a fratricide. The Egyptians traced it to the vengeance of their gods on the murderer of Apis. It appears from a passage in the Behistun Inscription [2] that a revolt of his army drove Cambyses to despair and suicide.

See Wiedemann, *Gesch. Ægyptens von Psammetich I. bis Alex. d. Grossen*, 227.

[1] It is doubtful whether this was a national rising of the Medes against the Persians (Spiegel, *Eranische Altertumskunde*, ii. 309), or, as Rawlinson (*Herodotus*, ii. 493) supposes, an attempt made by the priestly caste to wrest the supreme power from the soldiery.

[2] Spiegel, *Altpersische Keilinschriften*, 7.

The death of Cambyses without issue left the pretended Bardes in peaceable possession of the throne. It is stated in the Behistun Inscription that he governed with great severity, and in particular put to death a number of persons who had known the true Bardes, and were thus in a position to discover and expose the fraud by which he reigned. But the rule of the Magian seems to have been on the whole acceptable to the peoples of the empire.[1] They saw in him a son of the great Cyrus, that Bardes who had always been more popular than the tyrant Cambyses,[2] and quietly owned his sway. In order to ingratiate himself with his subjects, the pretender made proclamation throughout the empire that for a space of three years there should be exemption from payment of tribute and from military service—a measure of relief by which the Jews no doubt benefited, along with the other provincials. The reign of the Magian, however, was too short to have any direct bearing on the fortunes of the Jewish colony. In the

---

[1] 'He treated all his subjects,' says Herodotus, 'with such beneficence, that at his death all the people of Asia, except the Persians, regretted his loss.'—iii. 67.

[2] Spiegel, *Eran. Alt.* ii. 305.

eighth month of his usurpation a conspiracy was formed against him by seven Persian lords, who made their way into the palace, overpowered the guard, and dispatched Gaumâta with their daggers (521 B.C.). The chief of these conspirators was Darius, son of Hystaspes, with whom a new chapter of Jewish history begins.

CHAPTER VII.

Haggai.

IN his great Inscription, graven in three languages—Persian, Babylonian, Elamite—on the rock-face of Behistun,[1] Darius traces his descent from Achæmenes, through Teispes, the great-grandfather of Cyrus. He thus claimed the throne, not merely because his hand had slain the Magian, but because he belonged, like Cyrus, to the royal race of the Achæmenidæ—to the Persian branch of the line, while Cyrus had belonged to the Elamite. In the Inscription on his tomb at Naksh-i-Rustam Darius calls himself 'a Persian, the son of a Persian: an Aryan, the son of an Aryan'—which, by implication, Cyrus was not. And while Cyrus in his Inscriptions appears as a

---

[1] On the Behistun and other Inscriptions of Darius, see *Records of the Past*, i. and vii.; Spiegel, *Altpersische Keilinschriften;* Oppert, *Le peuple et la langue des Mèdes.*

polytheist, Darius represents himself throughout as an orthodox and zealous Zoroastrian. 'By the grace of Ormazd I am king. . . . Ormazd gave me the kingdom. . . . The temples which Gaumâta the Magian had destroyed I restored. . . . The kings who went before me have not done what I assuredly have achieved by the help of Ormazd.'

Now, for the first time, the monarch was a Persian *pur sang*, and a devout Zoroastrian. The mixed blood of Cyrus, his religious versatility, had enabled him to reconcile many differences in his own person, and so to bind together the empire he had made. With Darius it was different. The peoples saw in him the representative of one race and of one religion, and on all hands his right to the succession was fiercely contested. First Elam, the native kingdom of Cyrus, rose in arms against him; next the Babylonians declared their independence, under a leader who assumed the magic name of Nebuchadnezzar, and gave himself out as the son of the last native king. No sooner were these revolts put down than others followed, and during the early years of his reign (521-515 B.C.) Darius and his Persians were engaged in desperate fighting for their supremacy. Now in the very heart of the empire, now at its extremest outskirts, the fires of rebellion broke out again and again; and there were times when the issue hung in the balance, when the throne of the Achæmenidæ tottered, and it seemed as if the Persian monarchy were in the throes of dissolution.

Meanwhile the Jewish colonists were left in comparative peace. Their country lay outside the area of these convulsions and civil wars. If Egypt had risen in revolt the case would have been different; but the strength of Egypt had been so recently and thoroughly broken by Cambyses that now, while so many provinces were struggling to throw off the Persian yoke, this latest conquest of all submitted quietly to Darius. When the news reached Jerusalem that the so-called Bardes was dead, that another king reigned, and was still far from being firmly seated on the throne, it roused to vigorous action a party among the Jews which had never reconciled itself to the do-nothing policy of the Jewish leaders. During the reign of Cambyses this party had either been reduced to silence by the force of events, or else had spoken in vain; now, their voice was raised once more, and with a better chance of being heard. The men of this party —the progressists, the prophets and followers of prophecy—insisted on the rebuilding of the Temple as the first, the imperative duty of their countrymen. In their view, the work had been too long delayed; there had been culpable remissness on the part of the people and their chiefs, which the circumstances of the time only partially excused. They might, if they pleased, have made ironical comment on the zeal which had repulsed the Samaritans, but had not proved sufficient for the task it had refused to share with others. They held, and with perfect truth, that wanting the Temple, wanting the full restoration of the national worship, there could be for Israel only the fiction of a national life. They looked with utter scorn on the feeble attempts of the colony to establish itself with some degree of comfort and solidity at Jerusalem, while the vacant space on Moriah proclaimed the failure of their purpose and their hopes.

To the prophets—those inspired politicians, always on the alert to mark the signs of the times—the accession of Darius appeared as a heaven-sent opportunity, a call to instant action. The character of the monarch was as yet mere matter for conjecture, and though the fact of his Zoroastrianism may have been known, and an inference favourable to Jewish aspirations drawn from it, there could be no certainty that Darius, as ruler of the Jews, would revert to the earlier policy of Cyrus. The official heads of the community, discouraged and daunted by previous failures, made no attempt to approach the new King. The prophets did not counsel any step of that kind. With unerring insight they grasped the situation. The central authority was for the moment weakened, almost paralysed, by a wide-spread rebellion; the sovereign was battling for his throne; the empire was passing through a crisis. At such a time the Jewish colony might reasonably hope to be forgotten or ignored. The original permit of Cyrus had never been revoked; it was valid still. Let them act upon it; let them build, and dare the consequences. It would be time enough to defend their action when it was called in question; time enough to conciliate the favour of the Persian court when it showed signs of remembering their existence.

In the sixth month of the second year of Darius[1] (Elul, August, 520 B.C.) Haggai the Prophet stood forward as the spokesman of his party, and pressed these views on the chiefs of the colony, lay and clerical. Nothing is known of Haggai, outside of his special prophetic mission; that he was one of the aged men, now octogenarians, who had seen the Temple of Solomon and lived through the whole term of exile, has been inferred from a passage in his Book,[2] but is only an inference. Probably no more than a selection from the discourses of this Prophet has been preserved, and these are given only in bald outline; but they do not want character, and sufficiently explain the impression they made. Placed side by side with the great Prophet of the Exile, Haggai is dwarfed indeed. Beyond the Temple, he has almost no horizon. The eagle sweep of vision, the untrammelled flight into the infinite, the

---

[1] Hagg. i. 1.
[2] *Ibid.*, ii. 3. Ewald, *Propheten des Alt. Bundes*, ii. 516.

splendid idealism, are gone; prophecy has descended to the earth, has become everyday, practical, even short-sighted. Haggai's word to the people, the keynote of his preaching, is *Consider*. His appeal is made to conscience and common-sense, and is virtually limited to the duty of building the Temple. He is an ardent legitimist, a patriot who looks forward to an actual restoration of the Davidic monarchy; in language very slightly veiled, he holds out to Zerubbabel the hope of mounting the throne of his fathers.[1] The style of Haggai is in keeping with his prophetic vein. He has no graces of rhetoric, no wealth of language. His way of emphasising a point is simply to repeat it over and over again, at the risk of becoming monotonous. But to say that his 'diction is poverty-stricken and without true power,'[2] that it is 'weak and watery,'[3] is an over-statement of its defects. The best evidence that this Prophet had a power both of oratory and personality—a power which may still be felt in reading the condensed reports of his

---

[1] Hagg. ii. 21-23.
[2] De Wette-Schrader, *Einleitung*, 474.
[3] Gesenius, quoted by Köhler, *Weissagungen Haggai's*, 27.

speeches, and which must have been felt more strongly by those who heard them delivered in their original form—is, that he succeeded in swaying the minds of his hearers, and rousing them to the action he desired. The distinctive features of Haggai's style, his pithy interrogatives, his homely phrases, his blunt directness, even his catchwords, were just those most likely to be effective with a popular audience. The people at once recognised in Haggai a 'messenger of Jehovah.'[1] They felt themselves rebuked by his intense earnestness, impressed by his fearless candour. His prophetic mission, so far as it is recorded, covers a period of four months only. But these four months saw more progress made with the great work of the nation than the fifteen preceding years.

It was during the religious festival held on the first day of the month, the 'day of the New Moon,' that Haggai's voice broke the long silence of prophecy. His first words were spoken to Zerubbabel and Joshua, as representing the people, and answerable for their default.

---

[1] Hagg. i. 13.

Chiefs and people alike had fallen into the way of saying that things were against them, that they were a poor and struggling community, that the building of Jehovah's house must stand over till better days should come.[1] Haggai would have none of this excuse. He pointed to the significant contrast that lay under his eyes and theirs—the contrast between the unsightly heap of ruins on the sacred hill, and the fine houses which the citizens of Jerusalem had built for themselves.[2] Hitherto they had been considering their difficulties; let them henceforth consider their ways.[3] They had been striving to establish themselves prosperously in the land, and had failed; let them now hear the true reason of their failure. It was because they had thought of self first, and of God only second, busying themselves every one about his own house while Jehovah was left houseless.[4] Their present outlook was dark indeed; the harvests already reaped that year had been miserably poor, and those that were still to reap promised little better.[5] What was

---

[1] Hagg. i. 2.
[2] Ibid., 4.
[3] Ibid., 5.
[4] Ibid., 9.
[5] Ibid., 6, 9, 10, 11.

to be done? Haggai's answer came straight and sharp :—'Go up to the hill-country, fetch timber, and build.'[1]

One great lesson the Jewish people had learnt during the years of exile—to hear and to obey the voice of a Prophet. Haggai's words had an almost instantaneous effect. The Bene ha-Golah saw at once that this was the true way out of their difficulties; the needed impulse had been given, and the zeal of former days revived. Zerubbabel and Joshua found that they had once more a willing people at their back. Three weeks[2] after Haggai's first address, they had begun again to gather materials for the building, and had set their hands to the work. The Prophet stood by the builders, cheering them on.[3] 'Jehovah is with you,' was his message of encouragement.[4]

The walls began to rise; it became possible to form some idea of the finished appearance of the Temple. And now the same expressions of feeling which had marred the joy of the foundation-day, fifteen years ago, made themselves heard once more. Of the generation which had

---

[1] Hagg. i. 8. [3] Ezra v. 2.
[2] Ibid., 15.   [4] Hagg. i. 13.

seen Solomon's Temple a few survivors still remained, who were naturally held in high veneration, and whose words had weight with their countrymen. The lamentations of these aged men over the contrast between present and past, their reminiscences of ancient glories which could never be recalled, tended to dispirit the people, and raised in many minds the doubt whether the colony had not embarked on a task beyond its powers, whether its utmost efforts could ever raise a House worthy of Jehovah. To counteract this feeling of despondency, which had affected even the chiefs of the community, Haggai came forward with a second message, on a day just four weeks after the work had been resumed.[1] In this message the tone of reproof is dropped; the Prophet rallies the people and bids them work on in hope. 'Who is left among you,' he cries, 'that saw this house in its former glory? and how do you see it now? is it not as nothing in your eyes?'[2] To draw comparisons of that kind was simply taking the pith and marrow out of the national enterprise; there was no

---

[1] Hagg. ii. 1.   [2] *Ibid.*, 3.

time to waste in vain regrets over the past while the present demanded all their strength and courage.[1] As for the future, let them trust in Jehovah. The Word and Spirit of Jehovah abode still with His covenant people, no less than with their forefathers who came out of Egypt in the days of old.[2] For the moment Israel was without power, almost without place in the world; either oppressed by the Gentiles, or treated with a pitying tolerance more galling than oppression. But in times to come—those 'last times' in whose contemplation the Prophets of Israel found solace for the petty miseries of a commonplace present—there would take place that 'shaking of the nations,'[3] that tremendous revolution in the Gentile world, through which the historic mission of Israel would reach its glorious consummation. At that great day, and it was near, there would be no question of comparison between the First Temple and the Second. To this House, which the people were now raising with painful effort and in humble wise, all treasures of the Gentile world should come.[4]

---

[1] Hagg. ii. 4. [2] Ibid., 5. [3] Ibid., 6.
[4] '. . . desirable things of all nations.' Ibid., 7.

The silver and gold of the Gentiles were Jehovah's, and He would give them to adorn His earthly dwelling.[1] The glory of this second House would far transcend the glory of the first; and to His people who doubted whether their poor handiwork would find acceptance, Jehovah of Hosts sent this assurance by the mouth of His Prophet.[2]

A few weeks after the delivery of this address, perhaps under its influence, a colleague appeared at Haggai's side. This was a young member of the priestly aristocracy, Zechariah ben Berechiah, one of the new generation which had been born in Babylon, and which combined the fruits of Babylonian culture with the intense national feeling of the Jew. The grandfather of Zechariah, Iddo, was at this time head of one of the priestly houses which had followed Joshua from Babylon,[3] and thus his social position,

---

[1] Hagg. ii. 8.
[2] *Ibid.*, 9.
[3] Neh. xii. 4. It appears from Neh. xii. 16 that Zechariah succeeded Iddo in this position. The prophet is called in Zech. i. 1, 'son of Berechiah, son of Iddo;' in Ezra v. 1, vi. 14, 'son of Iddo.' Probably Berechiah predeceased his father, and from the fact that the dignity of family headship passed

apart from his prophetic vocation, gave him an influence over his countrymen. Zechariah far surpasses Haggai in breadth of view and fertility of ideas. The older prophet is thrown into the shade; the younger becomes a power in the community, and for the time its central figure.

Zechariah first came before the people as a prophet in the month Marchesvan (October). 520 B.C. Possibly, in spite of Haggai's glowing predictions of the future splendour of the Temple, the builders had grown less enthusiastic, under the depressing influence of those who had no praises save for the past. As a man of the new generation which had suffered so bitterly and was still suffering for ancestral guilt and folly, Zechariah had little admiration for the past, and little sympathy with those who admired it. Others might dwell with lingering regret on the vanished glories of Israel—he preferred to study the darker pages of the national history, and found there the true lesson for the present. There is a

---

in consequence directly to Zechariah, the latter is known to the Chronicler as 'son of Iddo.' That the prophet was a young man at this date is shown by Zech. ii. 4.

tone of almost angry impatience, a feeling of almost personal wrong, in the words of warning and menace with which he begins his ministry. 'Be ye not as your fathers,'[1] sums up his first message to the people. Jehovah had sent His prophets to their fathers, but the prophets had cried to deaf ears, and the wrath of Jehovah had been kindled.[2] That generation, people and prophets alike, had passed away, but not until the prophetic word had been accomplished in the experience of those to whom it had been vainly spoken. The retribution which they had thought to escape 'overtook' them, and then, too late, they saw and owned that the messengers of God had spoken truly.[3] Let this generation beware of repeating the mistake of their fathers. Let them turn unto Jehovah of Hosts, and He would turn unto them.[4]

The voices which had been exalting the past and decrying the present sank into silence for the time before this vigorous allocution. But the feeling of discouragement was not so easily dispelled. The harvests of the year had

---

[1] Zech. i. 4. [2] Ibid. 2. [3] Ibid. 5, 6. [4] Ibid. 3.

failed; now, in the ninth month (Chisleu, November), the people had been obliged to empty their granaries in order to sow their fields,[1] and were within almost measurable distance of famine. What was the meaning of the blight that seemed to rest upon the land? How were they to reconcile it with the utterances in which the prophets foretold fruitfulness and plenty? Was not theirs the holy land? Had they not in the midst of them the altar of Jehovah, on which the daily sacrifice was offered? Why was it that Jehovah withheld His blessing from their labours and their soil? — Haggai dealt in characteristic fashion with these questions which were stirring in the mind of the community. Choosing a day when the priests were engaged in some ceremonial function, with the populace gathered round them in the space that was to be the court of the Temple, the Prophet stepped forward, and asked instruction on two points of the Law. If a man carried holy flesh in the fold of his garment, and if by chance the garment touched

---

[1] Hagg. ii. 19.

any other article of food—bread, wine, or oil—did that article of food thereby become holy? The priests answered, No. Then again, if a person who had been polluted by contact with a dead body touched any article of food, did it thereby become unclean? The priests answered, Yes.[1] Haggai turned to the people, in whose hearing these questions had been asked and answered, and took up his parable. So it is with you, he said. Israel was the man bearing holy flesh in the fold of his mantle: in the midst of Israel was the sanctuary of Jehovah. But just as the mantle in which was wrapt the holy flesh had no power to communicate holiness to other things, so there was no necessary connection between the holiness and the fruitfulness of their land; their land was holy in virtue of the sanctuary, but the mere possession of the sanctuary could not ensure them abundant harvests of corn, wine, and oil.[2] The land was not in this sense holy; but neither, as they were almost ready to believe, was it unclean, laid under a curse. It was they, the people of Israel, who

---

[1] Hagg. ii. 12, 13.   [2] Köhler, *Weissag. Haggai's*, 94.

were unclean — unclean, because they had forgotten the first of all their duties, and neglected the building of Jehovah's House. So long as the Temple lay in ruins, the hand of Israel was as the hand of one that had touched the dead; all their building and planting, their very sacrifices on the altar, were unavailing; the tainted hand gave its taint to all with which it came in contact.[1] This was the secret of their hardships, of the bad seasons and poor harvests that had been the rule since the laying of the foundation-stone, fifteen years ago.[2] Now that they had set about the work in earnest, now that 'stone was being laid on stone in the Temple of Jehovah,'[3] better things might be looked for. They were no longer unclean in God's sight, and the work of their hands would prosper. They had lately sown their winter wheat; already the early rains were falling, and there was promise of a more abundant harvest. That promise would be kept. From that day Jehovah would bless His people.[4]

From the people, Haggai turned to the Prince. Either with a knowledge or a pre-

---

[1] Hagg. ii. 14.   [2] *Ibid.*, 16-19.   [3] *Ibid.*, 15.   [4] *Ibid.*, 19.

vision of the troubles in store for Zerubbabel, the Prophet sought to infuse into him something of that steadfast courage in which, it would appear, his character was deficient. Again was predicted that 'shaking of the heavens and the earth,' that internecine civil war among the Gentiles,[1] which the events then transpiring in the Persian empire naturally suggested to the Prophet's mind. In that near day of divine wrath and judgment Zerubbabel need have no fear. His own personal safety, the perpetuity of his royal line, are assured; he is as the signet-ring on the finger of Jehovah,[2] the precious thing which its owner never parts with, never lays aside by day or by night. Zerubbabel, like his great ancestor David, receives from Jehovah the title of honour 'My Servant.' Amid the crash of empires, the fall of thrones,[3] his kingdom and his throne stand unshaken. 'I have chosen thee, saith Jehovah of Hosts'[4]—these words, in which the patriot, the royalist speaks, at least as much as the seer—close the last recorded utterance of Haggai.

---

[1] Hagg. ii. 22.   [2] Ibid., 23.   [3] Ibid., 22.   [4] Ibid., 23.

CHAPTER VIII.

Zechariah.

THUS far any hindrance to the work had come from within the community itself; now, while the people were labouring zealously, and rapid progress was being made,[1] a check was threatened from without. The Jews had no doubt hoped to complete their Temple without the knowledge of the Persian authorities, who would then have to deal with an accomplished fact; and in this they might have succeeded but for the jealous vigilance of their Samaritan neighbours. No sooner had the Samaritans become aware of what was passing at Jerusalem than they hastened to denounce their rivals to the Persian governor of Abar-Nahara, the Trans-Euphratene.[2] The Jews, they alleged, were fortifying their city,

---

[1] Ezra v. 8.   [2] *Ibid.*, 3.

and building what professed to be a temple but was really more like a citadel;[1] an accusation which had never yet failed to serve its purpose.

The Persian governor, Tattenai, appears to have been newly appointed to his office by the new king: at all events, he was quite ignorant of Jewish affairs—ignorant even of the name of Zerubbabel or Sheshbazzar,[2] who, as pekhah of Judea, was under his jurisdiction. The reports laid before him seemed sufficiently grave to demand an inquiry on the spot; he came in person to Jerusalem along with other Persian officials and their retainers, and called the chiefs of the colony to answer for their proceedings. Behind the chiefs now stood the prophets, and they showed a bold front to their accusers. Questioned as to the wall they were building, they were able to convince the Governor that it was no military rampart,

---

[1] Josephus, *Ant.* xi. 4, sect. 6. The Chronicler does not expressly refer to the Samaritans in this connexion, but the 'Apharsachites' of Ezra v. 6 are mentioned in iv. 9, in the list of foreign peoples settled in Samaria. Shethar-Boznai (v. 6) may have been at this time sub-satrap or pekhah of Samaria. The name is Persian. Bertheau-Ryssel, p. 68.

[2] Ezra v. 4, 10.

but the simple enclosure of a temple. Questioned as to their warrant for carrying on this work,[1] they quoted the decree of Cyrus, and referred in proof of it to the vessels of the Temple which that king had restored to their keeping.[2] Tattenai judged the matter without prejudice, as a mere detail of administration. He had all a Persian official's respect for an edict of the Great King, a law of the Medes and Persians. He assured himself by personal inspection that no sinister purpose underlay the works now being carried on at Jerusalem. Accordingly, he did not take it upon him to interdict the building, but simply drew up a report in which he recited the circumstances of his visit to Judea, and asked that search might be made among the documents in the royal treasure-house at Babylon for that decree of Cyrus to which the Jews had appealed.[3]

The Jews were naturally elated at this result. It was a proof to them that the divine favour rested on their undertaking.[4] It added to the prestige of the party of prophecy, under whose impulse and direction the chiefs of the

---

[1] Ezra v. 9.   [3] Ibid. 17.
[2] Ibid. 14, 15.   [4] Ibid. 5.

community had acted in the matter. The work was now pushed on with greater vigour than ever. Already the beams that were to support the ceiling of the Temple had been fixed in the massive[1] walls, an evidence of the progress that had been made since the day of Haggai's first summons to action. One idea now possessed the people—to make the very most of the interval between the despatch of Tattenai's report and the decision of the Great King.

There was one means of influencing that decision, so fateful for the future of Judaism, to which the leaders of the colony would naturally have recourse. Their adversaries had been foiled, so far, but it was certain they would not give up the game; their charges and complaints would be carried from the throne of the satrap to the throne of the king. To the Jews it was of paramount importance that they should gain the king's ear, and

---

[1] Ezra v. 8. This passage mentions 'stones of rolling' as being used—*i.e.*, stones too massive to be moved otherwise than on rollers. The 'timber laid in the walls' refers probably to the beams (Reuss)—not to the inner lining or wainscoting of the walls (Schultz), as the work could scarcely have been advanced to that stage in the time.

neutralise the attempt that was being made to fix on them the stigma of disloyalty. To do that they must send an embassy to the Persian court; they must send their most prominent man.

The compiler of the apocryphal Book of Ezra has preserved a curious legend [1] in which Zerubbabel figures conspicuously at the court of Darius. The king had given a great feast to all the princes, satraps, and officials of his empire. On the night after the feast, while Darius slept in his bedchamber, three young men of the royal bodyguard agreed on a contest of wits—each was to write an aphorism, the writings were to be sealed and laid under the king's pillow, and on the morrow the king and princes of Persia were to decide which of the three had written the wisest sentence. The first wrote, Wine is the strongest. The second wrote, The king is strongest. The third wrote, Women are strongest, but above all things Truth beareth away the victory. Next morning King Darius found the writings, seated himself on his throne of judgment

---

[1] 1st Apoc. Ezra iii.-iv.

with all his courtiers and councillors about him, and called on the three young men to defend by argument the sentence each had written. The first then launched forth into praises of wine, the great leveller, 'which maketh the mind of the king and of the orphan to be all one,' and 'maketh every heart rich, so that a man remembereth neither king nor ruler.' The second lauded the power of the king, who is 'but one man,' yet is supreme over all; 'they slay and are slain, yet trangress not the king's commandment; if they get the victory, they bring all to the king.' The third spoke of the power of woman, illustrating his point by a piquant episode of which he himself had been an eye-witness at court;[1] and then proceeded to show that while women are stronger than wine, stronger than the king, yet Truth is strongest of all. 'Great is the earth, high is the heaven, swift is the sun in his course. . . . Is he not great that maketh these things? Therefore great is the Truth, and stronger than all things.' Then, it is said, all

---

[1] 1st Apoc. Ezra, iv. 29-31.

who heard the speaker approved of his words, and cried, 'Great is Truth, and mighty above all things'[1]—and the king bade him name his reward, for he had been found wisest. 'And he said unto the king, Remember thy vow, which thou hast vowed to build Jerusalem'—for this young man, according to the legend, was no other than Zerubbabel, Prince of Judah.

This whole passage is, of course, quite valueless as history. It must be taken as a popular tradition, worked up not unskilfully from the literary point of view, which the compiler of the apocryphal Book has fitted into his narrative with a daring disregard of the anachronisms involved.[2] The nucleus of his picturesque story, the simplest form of the popular tradition, may be found in the passing reference to Zerubbabel as one 'who spake wise sentences before Darius the King of

---

[1] The Vulgate rendering has, with a slight change, become proverbial—*Magna est veritas, et prævalet.*

[2] Fritzsche takes the passage as the working up of a popular tradition, which lent itself to a display of rhetoric; Zunz, as a mere draping of certain moral reflections, which the author of the Book found ready to his hand.—Fritzsche, *Handb. zu d. Apok.* i. 6.

Persia in the second year of his reign;'[1] and there is something to be said for the suggestion[2] that this speaking of wise sentences by Zerubbabel refers to the skilful conduct of his mission to the Persian court, the success with which he advocated the cause of his religion and country before the king. A comparison of the references in Haggai's Book with those in Zechariah's points to the conclusion that while Zerubbabel was present in Jerusalem down to the ninth month of the second year of Darius, he was, after that date, away from Jerusalem—presumably engaged in furthering the interests of his people at the Persian court, and using every effort to have the decree of Cyrus countersigned by Darius.[3]

Happily for the Jewish colonists, the absence of Zerubbabel did not leave them without a head, a man of power. It was not to the

---

[1] 1st Apoc. Ezra, v. 5, 6. This passage is corrupt; it makes 'Joacim the son of Zorobabel' the speaker, in contradiction to a previous statement (Apoc. Ezra, iv. 13). Zerubbabel had no son of that name (1 Chron. iii. 19, 20), and was himself evidently the original hero of the story.

[2] Herzfeld, i. 320.

[3] Derenbourg, *Hist. et. Géog. de la Palestine*, 21. Mention of an embassy of Zerubbabel is made by Josephus, *Ant.* xi. 4 sect. 9; and by Philo in his *Breviarium de Temporibus*.

High Priest Joshua, it was not to any of the elders of Judah, that the people looked for guidance and government; once again, and for the last time, as in the days of Ahaz, of Hezekiah, of Josiah, the Prophet was the foremost man in the state, the true representative and ruler of the community. Beside Zechariah the official chiefs of the colony are mere shadows; it is he who speaks to the people, acts in their name, decides the questions they bring before him; even dictates to the priests in matters of religious observance. In his symbolism, at once vivid and obscure, his exuberance of imagery, his elaboration of the fantastic, Zechariah resembles his greater predecessor Ezekiel; in form and style, both bear traces of Babylonian influence. In Zechariah the prophet has become a student. The generation to which he belonged had found its chief solace in the writings of the great teachers of the past; it was steeped in prophecy; and his Book shows the extent to which he had read and appropriated the literary treasures of his nation. His field of vision is wider than that of his contemporary; with him also the Temple stands in the foreground, but it does not, as with Haggai, shut out the prospect of the things beyond. Like Haggai, he is a staunch royalist, a devoted adherent of the House of David; but he is a priest as well as a patriot, and places the High Priest side by side with the Prince. In his teaching of religious and moral truths he rises far above his contemporary. The building of the Temple, the full restoration of the Mosaic ritual, are great matters to Zechariah, but greater still are the virtues of honesty and sincerity. As *censor morum*, he treads in the footsteps of the great prophets of the past.

In the eleventh month (Shebat) of the second year of Darius,[1] Zechariah unfolded to the people a series of seven visions of the night, with their interpretation and commentary. The psychology of these visions may be variously explained; how they were seen, in dream or trance, is immaterial. Evidently they embody the thoughts which were then agitating the minds of the people, of their leaders, and of the Prophet himself; they are the reflection and solution of doubts suggested by the circumstances of the present. As yet

---

[1] Zech. i. 7.

there was no sign of that 'shaking of the nations' which Haggai had foretold. The Gentiles were supreme in the world; Israel was still downtrodden and despised. Men were heard saying that the indignation of Jehovah had not yet spent itself; they were inclined to post-date the beginning of the seventy years of which Jeremiah had spoken, to argue that the Return had not closed the Captivity.[1] Zechariah's first apocalypse had reference to these doubts, raised by the contrast between the prosperity of the Gentiles and the adversity of Israel; doubts which extended even to the feasibility of building the Temple.[2] The Prophet finds himself in a valley of myrtle trees, and there beholds a vision of angels mounted on steeds of divers colours.[3] These angel-riders have gone to and fro throughout the earth; everywhere they have found peace and rest[4]—no symptom of that mighty political convulsion from which Israel was to emerge triumphant. Nevertheless the Prophet was bidden to say that the favour of Jehovah was with His own people, not with the Gentiles; that the afflictions of Israel would be avenged on its

---

[1] Zech. i. 12.   [2] *Ibid.*, 16.   [3] *Ibid.*, 8.   [4] *Ibid.*, 11.

oppressors; that the Temple and the City would be rebuilt, and the days of prosperity return.[1] The second vision represents the same idea. 'Four horns' are seen—the heathen powers that have broken and dispersed the chosen people; and again 'four smiths,' ready to shatter these horns, these powers.[2] Each destroying empire has its appointed destroyer; Israel is indestructible.

One cause of deep concern to the people in those days was the condition of Jerusalem—still in many parts ruinous, unwalled, and sparsely populated. The Prophet's third vision is a message of patience and confidence to his countrymen, who are grieving over the lamentable aspect of their city, and contrasting it despairingly with the Jerusalem of former days. He beholds a man with a measuring-line in his hand, going forth to measure the length and breadth of Jerusalem:[3] this man is the new Israel, intent on schemes for restoring the ancient grandeur of the city, and at the same time painfully conscious of their inability to make it what it had been. An Angel stays the hand that holds the measur-

---

[1] *Ibid.*, 15, 16.   [2] *Ibid.*, 18-21.   [3] Zech. ii. 1, 2.

ing-line. It was vain to think of measuring the Jerusalem of the future. No walls could contain that teeming population, which would overflow all bounds, and spread out in suburbs and villages till none could say where the city ended and the country began. No walls would be needed, for Jehovah would be a wall of fire round about Jerusalem, as well as a glory in the midst of her.[1] And then the Prophet turns to a quarter from which this increase of the people, in part at least, was expected to come. He echoes the old cry of the prophets before him: 'Ho, ho! flee from the land of the north! . . . Ho! Zion! deliver thyself, O dweller with the daughter of Babel!'[2] It seemed as if the Judeans had been forgotten by the Golah, who dwelt contentedly in Babylon, leaving the colony, the advanced guard of the nation, to fight its own battle without help or sign of sympathy from them. But Zechariah could not forget his countrymen beyond Euphrates, nor consent to any loosening of the bond that should unite the Israel abroad with the Israel at home. The political

---

[1] Zech. ii. 4, 5. [2] *Ibid.* 6, 7; *cp.* Isa. lii. 11; Jer. li. 6.

storm then brewing in 'the north country' had not escaped the Prophet's watchful eye. Babylon was not likely to be much longer the safe and pleasant dwelling-place which the exiles had found or made it. Already one revolt of the Chaldæans against Darius had been drowned in blood; a second war of independence was on the eve of breaking out,[1] a second reconquest of Babylon by the Persians would follow, and the Jewish inhabitants would have to share in all the sufferings and perils of the siege and capture of the city. Those might fare worse in the end who had shrunk from the hardships and poverty of Judea. Evil days were coming on Babylon; let the voluntary exiles who still lingered there arise and depart, and seek their true home. Zechariah's warning cry to the Golah closes in a more elevated strain. The spirit of the great Exile-Prophet still lives and finds voice in Israel. If Zechariah takes his symbolism from Ezekiel, he takes his catholicity

---

[1] Behistun Inscription. The second revolt of Babylon was headed by an Armenian named Arakha, who also, like his predecessor in rebellion, styled himself 'Nebuchadnezzar, son of Nabonidus.'

from the Babylonian Isaiah; and in face of the religious Chauvinism, the grasping exclusiveness of Jewish national feeling, proclaims the coming of a day when the Gentiles also shall join themselves to Jehovah, and Jew and Gentile shall be one people.[1]

Evidently the position of the High Priest in those days had been satisfactory neither to the community nor to himself. The pontificate, without the Temple, was anomalous; and there was the haunting fear that the office might never regain its ancient dignity; that even were the Temple rebuilt, it could never take the place of the former sanctuary, nor its chief minister be what his predecessors had been, from Aaron down to Zadok, from Zadok to Seraiah. Possibly, too, there may have been in Joshua's mind a sense of personal failure and shortcoming, a consciousness that he might have done more to fan the popular zeal and quicken the completion of the Temple. The fourth vision of Zechariah carried consolation to the High Priest, burdened with the feeling of his own and the nation's guilt. At

---

[1] Zech. ii. 11.

the bar of the Angel of Jehovah, Joshua stands arraigned. On his right hand is the Adversary, who lays accusation against him. He wears, not the spotless apparel of the High Priest, but 'filthy garments'—emblematic of the sin which cleaves to him and to the people he represents before Jehovah. The Adversary is rebuked; the soiled raiment is taken off the High Priest; a clean mitre and new robes are given him to wear.[1] It was a message of hope and encouragement to Joshua and his colleagues.[2] Priests and people had sinned, were sullied with impurity; but Jehovah had forgiven, in consideration of the terrible penalty endured in the past (for were they not as a brand plucked from the fire?)[3] and on condition of faithful service in the future. The High Priest need not fear for himself, for his office, or for his order. Zechariah sees clearly into whose hand the government of Israel must pass in the time to come. It is the High Priest who shall not only 'keep the courts' of Jehovah—preside over the worship of the restored sanctuary—but who shall also

---

[1] Zech. iii. 1-5.   [2] *Ibid.*, 8.   [3] *Ibid.*, 2.

'judge His house'—bear rule over Jehovah's people.[1]

But the Prophet, while giving this prominence to the High Priest, cannot part with the dynastic hope which clings to the person of Zerubbabel. His affection and sympathy, like those of all true patriots, followed the absent Prince who was facing difficulty and danger in the interests of his countrymen, and whose return was waited for with ardent longing. There were those in the colony who had lost faith in Zerubbabel, and who predicted the failure of his mission to the Persian court. They 'despised the day of small things;'[2] despised the part which the heir of their royal house played as a petty

---

[1] Zech. iii. 7. Ewald (*History*, v. 111) suggests as the historical basis of this vision that Joshua was at the time seriously compromised by accusations lodged against him at the Persian court. This is only less fanciful than Stanley's explanation: —'The splendid attire of the High Priest, studded with jewels, had been detained at Babylon, or, at least, could not be worn without the special permission of the King; and until the accusations had been cleared away, this became still more impossible. But the day was coming, as it was seen in Zechariah's dream, when the adversary would be baffled, the cause won, and the soiled and worn clothing of the suffering exile be replaced by the old magnificence of Aaron or of Zadok.'—*Jewish Church*, iii. 91.

[2] Zech. iv. 10.

provincial governor, a hanger-on at a foreign court; despised the efforts that had been made to rebuild the Temple, and the results that had been so far won. Zechariah has a vision which rebukes these detractors, and inspires with fresh hope the friends of the Davidic monarchy. He beholds the golden candelabrum of the Temple, seven-branched: two olive trees grow, one on either side of it: a branch of either tree, laden with ripe fruit, drops its oil into the fountain of the candelabrum, whence it flows to each of the seven lamps, feeding its flame.[1] The golden candelabrum is the community of the second Temple; the two olive-branches are the 'two anointed ones'[2]—Joshua and Zerubbabel. The Prince of David's house has his unction, his place in the economy of Israel, as well as the successor of Aaron. Zerubbabel's efforts on behalf of his people, feeble as they might seem, must not be despised; for this was the word of Jehovah: 'Not by might, and not by power, but by My Spirit, saith Jehovah of Hosts.'[3] The success of these

---

[1] Zech. iv. 2, 3; 11, 12.
[2] *Ibid.*, 14; Heb. 'sons of oil.'   [3] *Ibid.*, 6.

efforts must not be despaired of, for before Zerubbabel, God helping him, mountains of difficulty would become as level ground.[1] His hands had founded the new Temple, his hands would finish it; and those who now spoke slightingly of the Jewish prince would yet see him crown the great work amid the loud gratulations of a rejoicing people.[2]

But the mere completion of the Temple, which he looked upon and foretold as an absolute certainty of the near future, was not enough from Zechariah's point of view. The Temple was chief among the externals of Judaism, but it was an external, after all. The prophet of a previous generation had taken his stand at the gate of the former House, and uttered a solemn protest against those 'lying words'—'The temple of Jehovah, the temple of Jehovah, the temple of Jehovah is this'—had warned the people to 'amend their ways and their doings,' and not to imagine that the possession of the sanctuary would avert the judgment that follows dishonesty, injustice, and extortion.[3] True to

---

[1] Zech. iv. 7.   [2] *Ibid.*, 8-10.   [3] Jer. vii. 1-7.

the best traditions of the prophetic calling, Zechariah impresses the same lesson on his contemporaries. He had not, like his predecessors, to contend against idolatry; from that sin, at least, the new Israel was free. But the Jews, who had been taught the guilt and folly of idolatry in the school of exile, had unfortunately learned in the same school other lessons which had an evil influence on the national character. A state of servitude long continued naturally lowers the moral tone of a people; and though in the case of the Jews their religion counteracted this effect, it did not wholly prevent it. In religion they rose superior to their conquerors; in morality, particularly in commercial morality, they descended to much the same level. Their energies, debarred from other outlets by the loss of freedom, had been concentrated on the work of money-getting; and their residence in the great mercantile city, the London of the old world, had rubbed off what remained of the ancient simplicity of Jewish life, and destroyed the last vestiges of that ideal state in which no man was rich, and no man poor. The men of the Return were the least mercenary and materialistic of their nation, but even they were not taint-free. Petty, sordid vices, brought with them from the 'land of traffick,' disfigured the social life of the new community. Cases of theft, the use of false weights and measures, were not uncommon; and persons charged with these offences did not hesitate to forswear themselves before the judges in order to secure an acquittal.[1] Instead of that disinterested fraternal spirit which alone could enable the colony to offer a solid front to its difficulties, selfishness and uncharitableness prevailed; there was more readiness to make profit out of a neighbour's want or weakness, than to show liberality and offer help.[2] Such meanness and covetousness were revolting to the Prophet, and his generous indignation flamed out against those who thus brought scandal and danger on Israel. He had to repeat the warning, so often repeated, that no divorce was possible between religion and morality. The people were zealous in building the Temple, and ere long the

---

[1] Zech. v. 3. [2] *Ibid.*, vii. 9, 10; Neh. v. 1-13.

Temple would be built. But their zeal, their possession of the Temple, would be of no avail, so long as they lacked the elementary virtues of truthfulness, integrity, and brotherly kindness; and they need not think to honour Jehovah by building Him a House, while at the same time they dishonoured Him by swearing falsely in His name.[1] All these things pass before the Prophet in vision. He sees a great roll flying over the land, inscribed on one side with the curses pronounced against fraud, on the other side with those pronounced against perjury.[2] Again, he sees an ephah,[3] within which the figure of a woman is seated, having in her lap a leaden talent. The ephah represents the false measure, the talent of lead the false weight; the woman is Wickedness, which uses and profits by such things—the genius of unfair trade.[4] Two women, winged like storks, fly by, so swiftly it seems as though 'the wind were in their wings;' they snatch up the ephah, bear it aloft, and carry it

---

[1] Zech. v. 4.
[2] *Ibid.*, 1-3.
[3] The largest dry measure in use among the Jews, corresponding nearly to the English bushel.
[4] Zech. v. 6-8.

away to the land of Shinar (Babylon), there to be established in its proper place.[1] The use of false weights and measures, the tricks of trade, belong to Babylon, not to Judea. They are an ugly excrescence on the national life of Jehovah's people, which must be holy in itself, and not merely call itself holy in virtue of the Temple.

In his closing vision the Prophet's eyes are turned once more towards the North, and his thoughts go forth to the Israel which still dwells among the heathen. He sees the four winds of Heaven, under the semblance of chariots drawn by horses of different colours. From the mountains of Judah they speed on their course to all quarters of the world, bearing with them the Spirit of Jehovah. His gaze follows wistfully the chariot that passes north, till the comforting message comes to him: 'These that go forth to the northern land have made My Spirit to rest upon the northern land.'[2] There could be no more hopeful sign of the times than a revival of religious and national feeling among the Babylonian Jews, a 'resting of the Spirit of

---

[1] Zech. v. 9-11.   [2] Zech. vi. 1-8.

Jehovah' upon the Golah. The Jewish colonists had felt bitterly the neglect of their brethren beyond Euphrates, who might have done so much to aid them in their struggles, and had done so little. Zechariah assured his countrymen of a happy change in this respect. Even now the Israel abroad was being roused from its apathy. The thoughts of men were turning towards Jerusalem, towards the Temple. Their sympathy was being awakened; their gifts would come.

Ere long a tangible proof of this sympathy was given, and the expectations raised by Zechariah's visions of the night were fulfilled by an incident of the waking day. Three strangers arrived in Jerusalem—Jews of the exile, come as envoys and representatives of their people in Babylon, bringing gifts of gold and silver for the sanctuary. Zechariah saw at once the significance of this event, the possibility of turning it to account as a manifest fulfilment of prophecy and a stimulus and encouragement to the people. These deputies of the Golah were the harbingers of many yet to come; the offering they brought was but the first instalment of the treasure which should afterwards pour in to Jerusalem from her children in distant lands. In order to signalise this occasion, to impress its meaning on the popular mind, Zechariah did what only a prophet, a man owning no authority of this world, could have done. The three foreign Jews—Helem, Tobijah, and Jedaiah—had been hospitably received by one Josiah ben Zephaniah, a citizen of Jerusalem. Zechariah went to this man's house, and gave order that with part of the treasure brought from Babylon a crown should be made, a twisted fillet of gold and silver. Then, when the deputies had come before the chief priests to make formal presentation of their tribute, in sight of the people gathered round, the Prophet stepped forward, and set the crown on the head of Joshua the High Priest.[1] It was a strange act, and might

---

[1] Zech. vi. 10, 11. Ewald proposes to amend the text by inserting after ver. 11 the words 'and upon the head of Zerubbabel'—with the idea that two distinct crowns (the word in the original is plural) were made, one for each leader of the people. The context does not favour this emendation. Wright (*Zechariah and his Prophecies*, 148) remarks that in all probability the crown was placed on the head of the High Priest, rather than on that of Zerubbabel, because the former—not being of the house of David—would be less likely to misconstrue the Prophet's meaning. A more reasonable explanation

well fill the beholders with wonderment. Had, then, the sovereignty passed away from the ancient royal line for ever? Were all the hopes that had attached themselves to Zerubbabel now to be abandoned? Was the house of Zadok to supplant the house of David?—The Prophet's answer to such questions is veiled under a mysterious allusion to the Messianic time. For the moment there was a dual headship of the nation: a prince, without a throne; a high priest, without a Temple. Zechariah sees in the immediate future the restoration of the Temple, not the restoration of the throne; as a consequence, he sees the possibility of the high priest, not the prince, becoming the chief figure in the theocracy. But looking past all that, he foretells the coming of a time when the two offices shall be united in one Person— the Person of the Messiah, whose shall be at once the royal and the priestly throne.[1] The name he gives to the Messiah—*Zemakh*, 'the Branch,'[2]—is reminiscent of the promise made of

---

of the fact that Zerubbabel was not crowned is, that he was not at that time in Jerusalem. In any case, there were obvious political reasons against even a symbolic coronation of Zerubbabel.

[1] Zech. vi. 13.   [2] *Ibid*, 12.

old to King David and his posterity. But that promise did not depend upon the continuance of the ancient monarchy. Even though a king of David's race should never again sit on David's throne—and that was a possibility that must be taken into account—there would still exist in Israel an office that was typical of the Messianic office. That office was the High Priesthood; in the High Priest, no less than in the King, Israel might see a type of its Messiah. So much and no more was meant by the impromptu coronation of that day. Zechariah's action most accurately prefigured the future, but in its intention it was symbolic, not personal. The fillet of Babylonian gold had been set on Joshua's head; it was not to rest there. It was to be preserved in the new Temple as a memorial of the piety which had sent this offering to the sanctuary; of the men who had brought the treasure over so many leagues of desert; of the citizen of Jerusalem who had opened his house to these messengers of the Golah.[1] Their gift had a moral value

---

[1] Zech. vi. 14. *Read* 'and for the kindness of the son of Zephaniah'—as in margin of *R.V.* This 'dedication of the crown' was not forgotten in Jewish legend, as appears from

far above the material. It proclaimed the solidarity of the Jewish people at home and abroad. It heralded the approach of the day so often predicted, when 'those from far should come, and build in the temple of Jehovah.'[1]

---

a passage in the Mishna treatise *Middoth* (3, 8): And in the roof of the porch were fastened golden chains, upon which the young priests climbed up, and saw the Crowns. As it is said, "And the Crowns shall be to Helem, and to Tobijah, and to Jedaiah, and to Hen the son of Zephaniah, for a memorial in the temple of the Lord."' Hitzig supposes that the people had scruples about accepting gifts from their countrymen in exile, inasmuch as these were transgressing a divine command by not returning to their native land; and that the Prophet's object in the dedication of the Crown was the removal of these scruples. But there is no trace of any such feeling among the Jews of that day, when the largesses of Gentile kings were received with gratitude.

[1] Zech. vi. 15.

CHAPTER IX.

The Edict of Darius.

DURING all this time the Jews had been working in faith, not knowing what might be the final decision of the Great King. As the satrap had recommended in his report, search was made among the archives kept in the treasure-house at Babylon. The edict of Cyrus was not found there. But the Jews had sufficient influence at court to carry the matter further. It was known, either that certain state documents belonging to the reign of Cyrus had been removed for greater safety from Babylon to Ecbatana, the seven-walled city of the Medes, or that duplicates of these documents, traced originally on the clay tablets of Chaldæa, had been made on rolls of parchment[1] or papyrus, and stored in the Median capital. Search was renewed at Ecbatana; and

---

[1] Sayce, *Introduction*, 52.

there, in the muniment-house of the *Bira*, the fortress-palace where the Persian kings spent their summers, was found the edict, or a copy of the edict of Cyrus, in which he authorised and provided for the building of the Jewish temple.[1]

King Darius had now before him the document which clearly expressed the mind of Cyrus with regard to the Jews. It was natural that he should hold in respect the intention of the great founder of the empire, and desire to continue his policy even in minor affairs of state. Possibly he may have recognised between his own creed and that of Israel an affinity which induced him to look favourably on his Jewish subjects. Darius Hystaspes was not a syncretist of the type of Cyrus. With him, the Zoroastrian faith was an impelling force. His wars were, in one sense, wars against idolatry; in the Behistun Inscription he boasts that he has extirpated heresy, and counsels his successors to show a similar zeal. There is some reason to suppose that the Jews had at this time their representatives at the

---

[1] Ezra vi. 1, 2.

Persian court, either Zerubbabel himself or other Jewish officials; and by this channel a knowledge of what Judaism really was might easily make its way to the king. The worshippers of Ormazd might well be drawn towards the worshippers of Jehovah by a certain community of sentiment, opposed as both were to idolatry, and animated by a like feeling of hatred and scorn for the lubricity and cruelty of pagan rites. As soon as the Jews had succeeded in convincing the King that they were not rebelliously inclined, that there could be no political danger in acceding to their wishes, they were able to appeal to his sense of justice and his religious sympathies, with so much effect that he gave not only his consent but his active help to the building of the Temple. There was a precedent for this which shows that Darius may not have been actuated solely by feelings of sympathy in his treatment of the Jews. Soon after his accession to the throne he sent commissioners to Egypt, charged with the duty of restoring the Egyptian temples and providing for the wants of the priests.[1] It was a matter of supreme import-

---

[1] Duncker, *Gesch. des Alt.* iv. 530.

ance to Darius, with so many rebellious provinces on his hands, to maintain peace in those regions; the prudence of the statesman controlled the zeal of the iconoclast. His concession to the Jews may have been the outcome of policy at least as much as of sentiment.

The edict which Darius issued in confirmation of the edict of Cyrus must have surpassed the most sanguine hopes of the Jewish patriots. At last a king had arisen among the Gentiles who answered to the prophet's description, and showed himself a 'foster-father' to Jehovah's people. There is no reason to doubt the substantial accuracy of the edict as it is given by the Chronicler; a copy or précis of the document, laid up among the Temple archives at Jerusalem, may have been found available by the historian of a later day.[1] After recapitu-

---

[1] Grätz (*Gesch.* ii[b] 100) pronounces the report of the satrap and the edict of the King 'utterly spurious' and 'without any basis of fact.' This is to make too much of such quite evident indications of the hand of the Jewish transcriber as Ezra v. 8, where the satrap is made to speak of 'the house of the great God;' and Ezra vi. 12, where Darius is represented as invoking his curse upon all kings and peoples who should hereafter do injury to the house of 'the God who has made His name to dwell' at Jerusalem. A Zoroastrian, whose god had no earthly dwelling, would certainly not have used such

lating the original decree of Cyrus,[1] King Darius issued his special commands to the satrap of Syria and his subordinates. They were to keep away from Jerusalem and leave the colony to itself; the thing which above all others the Jews desired.[2] The satrap was to deduct from the royal tribute-money raised 'beyond the River' a sum sufficient to defray the costs of the building; and thereafter to supply the priests with all things necessary for the due maintenance of their ritual—with victims for the altar, and with the wheat, salt, wine and oil used in the various offerings prescribed by the Law.[3] Any tampering with

---

an expression, which Schultz (in Lange's *Bibelwerk, ad loc.*) allows to be 'so decidedly Hebrew in style that we may suppose the author did not impart the decree verbally, or that Darius made use of Jewish help in this entire affair.' Bertheau (p. 80) compares the closing words of the Behistun Inscription, where Darius invokes the judgment of Ormazd on whomsoever shall deface the figures and writing on the rock; possibly his edict as to the Temple may have had some such conclusion. The threat of punishment in vi. 11, to which Grätz objects, is to be taken as very much of a formula, a Persian way of saying *le roy le veult*. The introduction of the name of Artaxerxes in vi. 14 proceeds simply from the desire of the redactor, or copyist, to group together all the Persian kings who favoured the Jews, without any strict adherence to chronology.—Reuss, *Chron. ecclés.* 213.

[1] Ezra vi. 3-5. [2] *Ibid.*, 6, 7. [3] *Ibid.*, 8, 9.

the edict or opposition to its purpose was to be visited with the severest penalties—the offender, *more Persico*, to be crucified on his own rooftree, and his house 'made a dunghill.'[1]

From the date of this edict may be traced a change in the feeling and attitude of the Jews towards their Gentile rulers. The hope of regaining their national independence, though never given up, was tacitly laid aside; and the most ardent patriotism had to admit that there were compensations for the loss of liberty, under a despotism so benevolent as that of Darius. His generous treatment of the Jews, the respect he showed to their religion, evoked a feeling almost akin to loyalty, and so long as the Achæmenian dynasty lasted there was no attempt at rebellion in Judea. It wanted only a religious persecution to revive the old hatred of the Gentiles, the old longing for political freedom, in all its fierce intensity; but Darius and his successors were not persecutors, and they had on the whole contented subjects in the Jews.

---

[1] Ezra vi. 11.

Judaism under Darius was not merely a *religio licita*; it was actually established and endowed by the State. The providing of the daily oblation had been looked upon in former times as a special function of the king in Jerusalem;[1] it was now undertaken by the king in Susa, whom the Jews, by their acceptance of his bounty, virtually acknowledged as their sovereign. There seems to have been no scruples about receiving the royal gifts offered for the building and maintenance of the sanctuary; and without any violence being done to Jewish feeling, or any thought that the worship of Jehovah was thereby profaned, sacrifices were regularly offered and prayers made in the Temple for the long life of the Persian king and his family. Darius had stipulated that this should be done, and the precedent thus set continued in force to a later age.[2]

All hindrances to the building of the Temple, both external and internal, were removed by this edict of Darius. The suspicion and ill-will of Persian officialism changed at

---

[1] Wellhausen, *Prolegomena*, 82.
[2] Ezra vi. 10; 1 Macc. vii. 33.

once into active friendliness.¹ The straitened means of the colony, which had barely sufficed for the work, were now supplemented from the treasury of the Great King. The people went on with their sacred task in a new spirit of hopefulness, and the sounds of labour once more heard at Jerusalem rejoiced not only the Judeans, but also their countrymen who still dwelt in the land of exile. A fresh proof of the sympathy felt by the foreign Jews with their brethren of the Return, and of the interest they took in the progress of the Temple, was furnished by an incident which again brought Zechariah to the front, and gave him an opportunity of speaking certain home-truths to his nation, in Judea and out of it. On the fourth day of the ninth month of the fourth year of Darius (November, 518 B.C.), about two years after the promulgation of the edict of that king, another deputation from Babylon arrived in Jerusalem. Their object in coming was partly to present a votive offering to the Temple,² partly

---

¹ Ezra vi. 13.
² Zech. vii. 2, 'To intreat the favour of Jehovah'—Heb. 'to stroke the countenance of Jehovah.' The idea of offering

to obtain an authoritative decision on a question which had seemingly caused a difference of opinion among the Golah, or some community of the Golah. A custom had grown up during the years of exile of observing as public fasts certain days which were sadly memorable in the history of the closing years of the Jewish kingdom.[1] The anniversary of the day when the Chaldæans began the siege of Jerusalem, of the day when they captured it, of the day when city and temple were destroyed, of the day when the last hope of Judah fell in the person of Gedaliah—each had its place in the calendar of the Exile. Chief among these fasts, since the event it commemorated marked the climax of the

---

presents is contained in the idiom. Jewish commentators are almost certainly right in assuming that this embassy came from Babylon. The rendering 'And Beth-el sent' (R.V.) gives scarcely better sense than 'and they sent to Beth-el.' 'Beth-el' here is probably either a corruption of 'Bab-el,' or else not a place-name at all, but simply 'house of God,' as in A.V.

[1] *Suprà*, p. 13. Before the exile, national fasts were only occasional; during it, they became regularised, 'in the first instance, doubtless, in remembrance of the *dies atri* that had been experienced, and to some extent as a substitute, appropriate to the situation, for the joyous popular gatherings at Easter, Pentecost, and Tabernacles, which were possible only in the Holy Land.'—Wellhausen, *Prolegomena*, 112.

national misfortunes, was that held on the ninth day of the fifth month (Ab), the day when 'the heathen had entered the sanctuary' and given it to the flames. Year after year, this fast had been faithfully observed; it had become an institution of the Captivity. But now that the new Temple was rapidly nearing completion, and better days seemed at hand, the propriety of continuing this observance began to be called in question by some, at least, among the Jews of Babylon. It seemed out of place that they should be mingling their lamentations over the old Temple with their rejoicings over the new. It might even be that their mourning for the past was displeasing to Jehovah, as implying a doubt of the divine blessing which rested on the present, of the divine promise given for the future. In order to have these doubts solved, they sent two of their number, Sharezer and Regem-melech — Chaldæan names both, but borne by good Israelites—with their retinue to Jerusalem, to consult the priests and prophets there.[1] Zechariah, who was both

---

[1] Zech. vii. 3.

priest and prophet, but who wore the prophet's *addereth* above the priestly robe, answered their question from the prophet's point of view. He spoke, indeed, *to* the priests, rather than in their name, expressly stating that his message was meant for them, as well as for the people of Judea and the representatives of the Golah.[1] The true prophetic hatred of that soulless formalism which Zechariah evidently saw to be the danger ahead of the people, the true prophetic insistence upon integrity of heart as the only thing that can give a meaning and worth to outward observances, lent a tone of pathetic indignation to these last of his discourses. What did it matter, all their talk and disputing about fasts? Were they likely to please God by their fasting any more than by their feasting, so long as they did not humble their hearts? Let them beware of falling into the error by which their fathers had been undone. The prophets of former days had warned their fathers, as he, the prophet of this day, warned them, to judge with justice, to deal with their brethren in the

---

[1] Zech. vii. 5.

spirit of brotherhood, to show mercy to the widow and the orphan, the stranger and the poor.[1] Their fathers had turned a deaf ear and a refractory shoulder to the prophets; they had made their hearts hard as a diamond; hence their calamities, their dispersion among the heathen, and the desolation of 'the pleasant land.'[2] Now that Jehovah had returned to Zion and again made His dwelling in Jerusalem, His people might take comfort from the prospect of better things. The present were days of hardship and insecurity, which made Jerusalem no fit dwelling save for those in the full vigour of life—the time was coming when old men and women would sit peaceably in the streets of the city, each with staff in hand by reason of the weight of years. The present were cheerless days, Jerusalem was a joyless city—the time was coming when the sounds of merriment would be heard again, and the streets would be filled with happy children at play.[3] As an earnest of this promised blessing, the Prophet could point to that change for the better which had already passed over

---

[1] Zech. vii. 7-10; cp. Isa. lviii. 6, 7.
[2] Zech. vii. 11-14.   [3] Ibid., viii. 3-5.

the circumstances of the colony, since the day when they had set their hand strenuously to the building of the Temple. Before that day their misery had been extreme; now, their burdens were sensibly lightened and their efforts to establish themselves in the land had met with a measure of success. Henceforth the vine, the 'seed of peace,' would give its fruit, the earth would yield its produce, the heaven send down its dew; and as formerly it had seemed to the nations as though Israel lay under a curse, so now the manifest blessing of Jehovah would rest upon His chosen land and people. It was the purpose of Jehovah in these days to do good to Jerusalem, therefore her citizens need not fear.[1] Only—and here Zechariah comes back to the special warning for which no doubt he saw special need—they must not think of the Temple as sanctifying Jerusalem and the people. Jehovah required personal holiness in those who served Him. It was they themselves, not the Temple or the want of it, that made holy or unholy the land. Let each man speak the truth and deal honestly with his neighbour.

---

[1] Zech. viii. 9-15.

Let even-handed justice be administered in the gates. Let there be no swearing of false oaths, for that was a thing hateful to Jehovah.[1] They themselves, by their love of truth and peace, would bring in the better time. Then there would be no further controversy about fasts. The four fast days of the Captivity would abrogate themselves; if remembered at all, they would be transformed into days of gladness and seasons of joy.[2] With a remarkable prediction of the future power of Judaism over all mankind, the voice of Zechariah falls silent—his mission, so far as it stands on record, reaches its close. 'Thus saith Jehovah of Hosts, Yet shall there come peoples, and citizens of great cities; and the citizens of one city shall go to those of another, saying, "Let us go speedily to intreat the favour of Jehovah, and to seek Jehovah of Hosts: I will go also." . . . Thus saith Jehovah of Hosts, In those days shall ten men take hold, out of all the languages of the nations, even take hold of the skirt of him that is a Jew, saying, "Let us go with you, for we have heard that God is with you."'[3]

---

[1] Zech. viii. 16, 17. [2] *Ibid.*, 19. [3] *Ibid.*, 20-23.

CHAPTER X.

The Second Temple.

WITH such words of promise sounding in their ears, the builders toiled on zealously, and took no rest until the Temple was completed. A record was kept of the precise day when the last finishing-touch was put to the work: it was the third day of Adar, the last month of the sixth year of Darius (February, 516 B.C.)[1] Just seventy years had passed since the destruction of the former House; twenty years since the laying of the foundation-stone by Zerubbabel; four years since the second and real beginning of the work, under the impulse given by Haggai.

The joy of the people over this fortunate issue of their labours, reached after so many delays and in face of so much discouragement,

---

[1] Ezra vi. 15.

found expression in the solemn dedication of the new Temple. This ceremony was made the occasion of a national festival, the first during twenty long and gloomy years. From all parts the Bene ha-Golah gathered to Jerusalem, with feelings of deepest thankfulness as they saw the height of Moriah crested once more with the gleaming walls of the sacred building which assured them of the guardianship of the Eternal. At the dedication of the former House, King Solomon had sacrificed sheep and oxen by the thousand, innumerable.[1] The 'day of small things' had to content itself with a humbler tale of victims. A hundred oxen, two hundred rams, and four hundred lambs, were brought that day to the altar, with—most significant offering of all—twelve he-goats, as an expiatory sacrifice for the twelve tribes of Israel.[2] It was a proclamation of the unity and indivisibility of Israel, an admission that the Temple of Jehovah, the centre and pivot of the national life, belonged not to any section of Israel, but to Israel as a whole. Though the vast

---

[1] 1 Kings viii. 5, 63.   [2] Ezra vi. 17.

majority of the assemblage in the sacred courts that day belonged to the Two Tribes of Judah and Benjamin, there were doubtless representatives present, in less or greater number, of the other Ten. But the twelve-fold offering had a meaning that went deeper and further than such partial representation. It expressed the hope of that greater Return, foretold by the Prophets, when the 'holy flock,' now scattered abroad and afar, should be gathered in complete to the fold at Jerusalem.[1]

Along with the smoke of the sacrifices on the day of dedication rose the strains of music and the voice of praise, which from this time onward formed an integral part of the Temple service.[2] There is no statement as to what psalms, newly composed, or chosen for their fitness from the ancient anthology, were chanted by the sons of Asaph during the solemnities of the day. Among older psalms, the 24th—among recent additions to the

---

[1] Ezek. xxxvi. 38.
[2] Ewald (*Hist.* v. 112) justly remarks that 'the Temple music . . . must have received a fresh impulse along with the complete restoration of the ancient service.'

psalter, the 118th, may very probably have been used on this occasion. Both are songs of dedication, and their lofty numbers not only express the triumphant, hopeful spirit naturally called forth by the ceremony—they almost picture the ceremony itself, the rolling back of the Temple gates, the joyous thronging of the courts, the priestly procession, the outbursts of choral singing, the solemn sacrificial rites performed in view of the people:—

> 'Lift up your heads, O ye gates,
> And be ye lifted up, ye everlasting doors,
> And the King of Glory shall come in.
> Who is the King of Glory?
> Jehovah strong and mighty,
> Jehovah mighty in battle.
> Lift up your heads, O ye gates,
> Yea, lift them up, ye everlasting doors,
> And the King of Glory shall come in.
> Who is this King of Glory?
> Jehovah of Hosts,
> He is the King of Glory.[1]'
>
> . . . . . .
>
> 'O give thanks unto Jehovah; for He is good:
> For His mercy endureth for ever.
> Let Israel now say,
> That His mercy endureth for ever.

[1] Ps. xxiv. 7-10.

Let the house of Aaron now say,
That His mercy endureth for ever.
Let them that fear Jehovah now say,
That His mercy endureth for ever . . .
Jehovah is my strength and song;
And He is become my salvation.
In the tents of the righteous is the voice of rejoicing and salvation;
The right hand of Jehovah doeth valiantly,
The right hand of Jehovah is exalted. . . .
Open to me the gates of righteousness;
I will go in by them, I will give thanks unto Jehovah.
This is the gate of Jehovah;
The righteous shall go in by it. . . .
Blessed is he that entereth in the name of Jehovah;
We have blessed you out of the house of Jehovah.
Jehovah is God, and He hath given us light:
Bind the sacrifice with cords, even unto the horns of the altar.
Thou art my God, and I will give thanks unto Thee:
Thou art my God, I will exalt Thee.
O give thanks unto Jehovah, for He is good;
For His mercy endureth for ever.[1]"

The first care of the spiritual chiefs of Israel, after the completion and dedication of the Temple, was the reorganisation of the priesthood, for which there was now an immediate necessity. During the twenty years that had passed since the Return, the functions of the priests had been limited to the ministry of

---

[1] Ps. cxviii. 1-4; 14-16; 19-20; 26-29.

the altar. Probably only a relatively small number of them had been resident in Jerusalem, the great majority being obliged to seek the means of livelihood elsewhere. But now that the sanctuary was restored and the ancient ritual re-established, there was work for all grades of the hierarchy, and the daily presence of numerous ministrants was required. The priests were now, as of old, arranged in their classes, the Levites in their sections,[1] each class and section taking the duties of a week, and being relieved on the Sabbath by its successor in regular order. The burden of supporting the priesthood, which must otherwise have pressed heavily on a community barely able to support itself, was lightened for the present by the generosity of the Persian king.

A special effort had doubtless been made to have the Temple finished before the year closed, in order that the feast of the passover might be fittingly observed on the appointed day in the first month of the new year (Nisan, March, 515 B.C.). Due preparation having

---

[1] Ezra vi. 18.

been made, priests and Levites having purified themselves from all taint of ceremonial uncleanness,[1] the people once more assembled at Jerusalem to celebrate the ancient feast in the ancient way. For three generations Israel had kept no passover until now, and the circumstances of the present time, no less than the associations of the past, heightened the significance of this first festival of the second Temple. The seven days' feast of unleavened bread was a season of rejoicing in Jerusalem. Something of the old cheerful, hopeful spirit came again into Jewish life; this might be, it was, only a passing gleam of prosperity, but the people sunned themselves in it all the more gratefully for the long period of suspense and struggle through which they had passed. 'Jehovah had made them joyful.'[2] The favour shown them by their Gentile ruler was itself a proof of the divine blessing.[3] Another such proof was the almost immediate effect of the restoration of the Temple and its worship upon the Israel which still, in its own land, dwelt with the heathen. The love and longing for

---

[1] Ezra vi. 20. [2] *Ibid.*, 22. [3] *Ibid.*

Jerusalem, once more the holy city, revived in the hearts of many of these lapsed Israelites; and, 'separating themselves from the filthiness of the peoples of the land,' they sought and obtained permission to eat the passover at Jerusalem with their brethren who had returned from exile.[1] This 'gathering together of the outcasts of Israel'[2] added not a little to the joy of the feast—to the general feeling of elation and confidence which inspired the sacred poems of that day, the psalms that bear in the Septuagint the names of Haggai and Zechariah.[3]

Curiously little is known as to the structure and dimensions of this second Temple, which stood for five hundred years as the centre of Jewish religious life, till it finally disappeared in

---

[1] Ezra vi. 21. The term *Nibdalim* ('they who separated themselves') used in this passage is referred by Geiger (*Urschrift*, 71) to the party within the community itself which thus early distinguished itself by greater strictness in the observance of the Law—in brief, the Pharisees. But the *Nibdalim* (*suprà*, p. 67) are said to have separated themselves 'from the filthiness of the Amme ha-Aretz'—not from the comparative laxity of other Israelites. They were descendants of the 'undeported' of both kingdoms, who had fallen into heathen ways, but who now returned to their ancestral faith and rallied to the common centre. See Wellhausen, *Pharisäer und Sadducäer*, 77.

[2] Ps. cxlvii. 2.   [3] Ps. cxxxviii., cxlvi-cxlix.

the 'restoration' undertaken by King Herod. The building is left wholly undescribed by the canonical writers, save in one passage,[1] which is too obscure to be of much value. For an idea of its size, architecture, and internal arrangements, one has to depend upon the analogy of the first Temple, the references in Josephus, and the traditions of the Rabbis. Apparently the Temple of Zerubbabel at least equalled that of Solomon in length and breadth,[2] and in the area covered by its courts. The artificial plateau formed on the summit of Mount Moriah was surrounded by a lofty wall, four-square, pierced with five gates, two on the southern, and one on each of the three remaining sides. Over the eastern gate, that by which pilgrims usually entered the sacred precincts, was placed a sculptured representation of the city of Susa, the chief

---

[1] Ezra vi. 3, 4.
[2] No doubt in height also, though Josephus (*Ant.* xv. 11, 1) states the contrary :—'Our fathers, truly, when they returned from Babylon, built this temple to Almighty God, yet it wants sixty cubits of its height, for by so much did that first temple which Solomon built surpass this temple. But let not any one condemn our fathers for negligence or want of piety herein, for it was not their fault that the temple was no higher.' In this statement, Josephus is misled by 2 Chron. iii. 4.

capital and favourite residence of the Persian kings [1]; either by royal command, as a kind of government mark, or more probably as a spontaneous expression of gratitude on the part of the Jews for the favours shown them by the Achæmenian dynasty. This entrance, afterwards called the Beautiful Gate,[2] and now the Golden Gate, was long known, from its distinguishing ornament, as the Gate of Shushan. Passing through any of these gates, one stood in an open space built round with cloisters— the outer court or Court of the Gentiles, which was not considered as holy ground, and which consequently was open to foreigners and to Jews who were for the time ceremonially unclean. A low wall or partition (Soreg), with gates at intervals, marked the limit beyond which no Gentile or defiled person might pass. Beyond the Soreg a flight of twelve steps led up to a broad terrace reserved for female worshippers, and known as the Court of the Women; and from this point, by another flight of steps, one reached through a massive gateway a second and still higher terrace, which formed the Inner

---

[1] *Middoth*, 1, 3. [2] Acts iii. 2.

or Upper Court of the Temple. It was on the broad sweep of the stairway leading to this court that the Levitical choristers and musicians took their stand during the daily service. The laity had access to the Inner Court, but only to a certain distance. This was marked by a barrier, so low that it did not interfere with the view of the people, beyond which was the Court of the Priests, where no layman might enter. To the north, in this court, stood the altar of burnt-offering, hastily erected in the first days of the Return; to the south, a great laver for the use of the officiating priests. Westward, and on ground still higher, stood the Temple itself, approached by a portico, and divided, like the Temple of Solomon, into greater and less—the Holy Place (Hechal), and, behind it, the Holy of Holies. A triple tier of side-buildings, flanking the outer walls of the sanctuary, contained chambers or cells for the priests. Above these wings, which were lower than the main building, were the windows that lighted the Hechal; whether there were windows to the Holy of Holies is uncertain. It is not at all likely that architecturally the second Temple had ' a certain resemblance to the buildings of Susa and Persepolis.'[1] Its designers most probably aimed at a reproduction from memory of the Temple of Solomon, with only such modification and enlargement as experience had shown to be needful.[2]

The second Temple, like the first, was a small building, and architecturally neither beautiful nor impressive. Indeed, the side buildings annexed to it, so far as their appearance can be judged from the confused statement of the Chronicler,[3] must have given a somewhat bizarre effect to the whole. The one thing that made the Temple outwardly imposing was its site on the hill-top: after passing the outermost wall of the enclosure, one still mounted continually from terrace to terrace, until the sanctuary was reached, crowning the steep ascent. The generation which raised

---

[1] Rosenzweig, *Jahrhundert*, 48.
[2] On the north side of the Temple enclosure was the fortress known as the *Bira* (a word of Persian origin, signifying 'castle'; in its later, Greek form, *Baris*) which Herod afterwards rebuilt and named Antonia. Nehemiah (ii. 8) refers to this building as 'the castle (*Bira*) which appertains to the Temple,' so that it must have been erected at least before his day.
[3] Ezra vi. 4.

this fabric took a natural pride in their handiwork; it represented to them much labour and self-sacrifice, and success won after the hope of success had been almost given up. But the generations which followed had no personal feeling of this kind, and the deficiencies of the new sanctuary were remembered long after the hard struggle of its builders had been forgotten. Of Solomon's Temple men had spoken proudly and fondly as 'our beautiful House,' 'the beauty of Israel;'[1] its successor did not call forth the same enthusiasm. The second Temple was felt to be at once less glorious and less sacred than the first. The shrill sounds of lamentation heard on the day when it was founded, and again and again during the years of its building, ceased with its completion; but the feeling of disappointment and failure provoked by the contrast between past and present never wholly died away, and found frequent expression in later times. If the post-exilian Temple did not fall short of its predecessor in size, it must at all events have been inferior

---

[1] Isa. lxiv. 11, lx. 7; Lam. ii. 1.

in massiveness, in finish, and in ornament. King Solomon, with all the resources of a prosperous kingdom at his command, had spent nearly eight years in building his Temple; half of that time sufficed to build the Temple of Zerubbabel. The rich magnificence of decoration in the former House, the lavish use of gold and of timber scarcely less precious than gold, on which the historians of Israel loved to dwell, were quite beyond the means of the Bene ha-Golah; and the author of Chronicles, who revels in details of past splendours, gives not a word of description to the humbler sanctuary of his own day.

But it was not merely in respect of outward adornment that the new Temple fell short of the old. It wanted that element of the supernatural, those signs of the divine presence, by which, according to ancient tradition, the former House had been visibly marked out as the earthly dwelling of Jehovah. There were things that could be, and were, restored. Once again, in the Heehal, stood the golden altar of incense, the golden table of shewbread, the golden candelabrum. Once again the High Priest assumed the robes and insignia of his office—the ephod, the breast-plate, the mitre, the fringe of golden bells. But behind the mysterious veil of the Temple was an empty Holy of Holies; and the High Priest, when he passed within the veil, wore no longer on his breast the Urim and Thummim, and no longer read the Yes or No of the Eternal in the shifting lights of the flashing gems.

It was characteristic of the early days of the Return, while the people were still in the first flush of enthusiasm, that men looked forward hopefully to a time when there should 'stand up a Priest with Urim and with Thummim.'[1] This hope had to be given up, like many more. It was strange, indeed, that it should ever have been entertained, for the mystic jewel had certainly fallen into disuse centuries before the Exile, there being no need for the High Priest to practise divination while the Prophets were there to declare the purpose of Jehovah. That the children of the captivity should have expected the restoration of the oracle shows how much their thoughts dwelt in a legendary past; that they made no attempt to restore it [2]

---

[1] Ezra ii. 63.
[2] Josephus (*Ant.* iii. 8, 9) asserts that the oracular jewel was

shows how they came to realise the practical limitations of the present.

'In the Holy of Holies,' says Josephus, 'there was nothing at all.'[1] When the Roman general, centuries after, drew aside the veil, he found the inmost sanctuary as it had stood from the times of Zerubbabel and Joshua—*vacuam sedem et inania arcana*.[2] There was no Ark of the Covenant in the second Temple. Nothing was ever known as to what finally became of the historic chest of gopher wood, which had been fashioned under the eyes of Moses, and to enshrine which worthily had been King David's primary motive in design-

---

in use during the great days of the Maccabees, and only ceased to shine in the second century B.C. But Jewish tradition is quite distinct on this point, that the Oracles were wanting in the second Temple. 'According to Jewish tradition, a Bath Kol, or holy echo, supplied the place of the departed Urim and Thummim, and of oracles long since silent. . . . The Bath Kol, which signifies "daughter of a voice," was a kind of divine intimation, which was as inferior to the oracular voice proceeding from the Mercy Seat as a daughter is supposed to be inferior to her mother. It was said to be preceded by a clap of thunder. This, however, was not always the case. . . . The Bath Kol seems to have been a sort of divination practised with the words of Scripture, like the Sortes Virgilianæ among the heathen.'—Barclay, *The Talmud* 16.

[1] *De bell. iud.*, v. 5, 5.   [2] Tacitus, *Hist.* v. 9.

ing a temple at Jerusalem. Possibly the Ark may have been secreted in some place of security, the clue to which was afterwards lost; probably it was destroyed, along with whatever it contained, when the Chaldæan soldiery looted and fired the Temple. No mention of it is made in the list of precious things taken to Babylon.[1] The mystery surrounding its fate gave rise to the wildest legends in after times. According to one tradition,[2] the great prophet Jeremiah, being warned by God, rescued the Ark from the destruction of the Temple, bore it far away to Mount Nebo, and hid it in a cave of the rocks—there to remain 'unknown, until the time that God should gather His people again together.' Some held that it had been actually taken to Babylon, in fulfilment of the prophecy, 'Nothing shall be left, saith Jehovah;'[3] others, that it had been hidden under the floor of the Holy of Holies. But the favourite legend of all was that, variously given in the Mishna and the Gemara, which made King Josiah, foreseeing the calamities of the future, hide

---

[1] Jer. lii. 17-23. [2] 2 Maccab. ii. 4-8. [3] 2 Kings xx. 17.

the Ark of the Covenant for safety somewhere in or near the wood-store of the Temple, in which place it still lay buried, manifesting its presence by unmistakable signs.[1] A tradition of the Rabbis has it that the place of the missing Ark in the second Temple was taken by a wonderful stone, 'which had been there from the days of the first Prophets, and which was called *Sattija*, "foundation-stone," standing three fingers'-breadth above ground.'[2] On this stone the High Priest is said to have rested the censer which he carried with him into the Holy of Holies on the day of Atonement.

---

[1] 'Once,' it is said, 'a priest employed near the wood-store noticed that the plaster on a particular spot differed from all the rest; he went to inform his companions, but died before he had time to finish the story: thus it became known that the Ark was stowed away there.' According to another tradition of the Rabbis, there were once two priests looking over wood in the wood-store, to see if any of it were worm-eaten (it being unlawful to use for the altar wood that was at all worm-eaten). One of these priests accidentally dropped his axe, and as it happened to fall on the place where the Ark was concealed, a fire instantly came forth and consumed him on the spot.—Hershon, *Treasures of the Talmud*, 32, 34.

[2] Mishna, *Joma*. 'Supposed by some to be the *Sukhrah* in the present Mosque of Omar. From its position, however, it seems more probably to have been the foundation of the altar of burnt-offerings.'—Barclay, *The Talmud*, 127.

Other things were regretfully remembered as belonging to the old sanctuary and wanting in the new,[1] but the absence of the Ark, with the Cherubim and the Shekinah, was seized upon by the popular imagination as the most significant of all. Before the first Temple was destroyed, Ezekiel had seen in vision the Glory of the God of Israel rise up from the cherubim, pass to the threshold of the Hechal, and thence depart;[2] it was an abandonment without any visible return. To the prophets and those who thought with them, the want of these symbols had its compensations. Jeremiah had looked forward to a day when the Ark itself, the most sacred of the national possessions, should be absolutely forgotten; and when Jerusalem—the holy people, not the Ark—should be called the throne of Jehovah.[3] In their conception of a spiritual worship the prophets were far in advance of their age; where they saw gain, others saw loss, and for a long time nothing more. But the centuries that followed

---

[1] Among them, the sacred fire which was said to have descended from heaven at the dedication of Solomon's temple, and devoured the sacrifice.

[2] Ezek. ix. 3; x. 18.   [3] Jer. iii. 16, 17.

were marked by a certain approach to the prophetic point of view. The new ritual was simpler, the new worship more direct than the old. Zerubbabel's House was never an object of superstitious devotion, to the extent that Solomon's had been in the past, or that Herod's afterwards for a brief period became. So long as the sacrificial system lasted, the temple at Jerusalem was the necessary centre of Jewish religion, but there were now spiritual wants which the temple could not satisfy. New tendencies set in, new institutions were developed, unchecked by any sentiment of fanatical reverence for a sanctuary which was felt to be incomplete and provisional. The very defects of the Temple, though at first bitterly regretted, had in the end a wholesome influence on the religious thought and life of Israel. The empty Holy of Holies pointed forward to the 'worship in spirit and in truth.'

CHAPTER XI.

The End of a Dynasty.

THE Temple was completed in the sixth year of Darius (516 B.C.)—the same year[1] in which that monarch carved the record of his victories over the nine rebels on the rock of Behistun. After this, Jewish history is left blank for a period of thirty years, the remainder of the reign of Darius (516-485 B.C.). It was a period crowded with great events. One Persian army passed eastward to the Indus, and made the Punjaub a Persian province. Another, led by the King in person, crossed the Bosphorus into Thrace, and marched from the Danube to the Don, driving the Scythian hordes before it. These expeditions did not content Darius. Cyrus had extended the empire in Asia, Cambyses in Africa; Darius strove

---

[1] *Journal of Asiatic Society*, xi. 189 ff.

to extend it in Europe, by the conquest and annexation of Greece. This attempt led to the sole failure of a long and prosperous reign. Darius found in the Greeks foemen of a different stamp and temper from any he had hitherto encountered, and his arms, invincible in Asia, met with crushing defeat at Marathon (490 B.C.). The King, old as he was, resolved on taking the field in person, and retrieving the ill-fortune of his generals. But in the midst of his vast preparations for a new invasion of Greece, the news came that Egypt had revolted; and before he had time to turn against either adversary, Darius died, in the thirty-sixth year of his reign (485 B.C.).

The Jews of Judea were not greatly affected, if at all, by the foreign policy of Darius. They lay outside the area of his wars, and may possibly never have heard of the great battle which decided the course of modern history. While Athens stands out in glorious publicity as protagonist of the West against the East, Jerusalem lies in the background of the time, unregarded and obscure. The internal administration of the empire under Darius concerned the Jews more nearly than his foreign campaigns. That king, the most able and enlightened by far of his dynasty, had no sooner succeeded in pacifying the empire than he set himself to organise its government and finances. The genius of Darius originated that so-called 'satrapial system' which remained ever after a feature of the Persian monarchy. His vast empire, extending 'from India to Ethiopia,'[1] was divided into between twenty and thirty great provinces, each under a satrap or governor-general, who was commonly a kinsman or favourite of the king. The satrap was responsible for the peace and good order of his province, and for the collection of the annual tribute, the amount of which in every case was fixed by royal decree. He had at his side two officials appointed by the crown—one a soldier, in command of the Persian garrison; the other a civilian, with the title of secretary, whose duty it was to report directly to the king, and thus act as a check upon the power of the satrap. Each province was sub-divided into *medinoth* (revenue districts), over which were set *pekhoth* (local governors), the chief duty of the *pekhah* being to collect the taxes of his

---

[1] Esther i. 1.

district, and pay them into the satrapial exchequer. These fiscal measures of Darius gained for him among the Persians, who despised everything that savoured of trade, the sobriquet of 'the huckster.'[1] They were however a boon to the provincials, who had hitherto been plundered, rather than taxed, in the king's name.

Under the satrapial system, the position of the Jewish colony in the Persian empire was exactly defined. Syria, with the island of Cyprus, formed a satrapy, of which the seat of government was probably at Damascus. Of this great province Judea was a humble *medinah*[2] or revenue district, under a *pekhah* who took his orders from the satrap of Syria. The condition of the Jewish colonists seems to have been fairly prosperous in the days of Darius. They shared in the benefits which his wise and firm rule conferred upon the empire at large. They were not overburdened with taxation. Above all, within certain limits, they were allowed to govern themselves. Persian ad-

---

[1] 'The Persians,' says Herodotus (iii. 89), 'called Darius a huckster, Cambyses a master, and Cyrus a father.'

[2] To the Jews, at home and abroad, '*the* medinah.'— Neh. . 3 ; Eccles. v. 8.

ministration was not inspired by any rage for uniformity. The satrap must be obeyed, the king's tribute paid to the last daric, the military contingent furnished to the last man, but the people of any province or district which discharged these duties promptly and peaceably, and kept on good terms with the Persian local authorities, might retain its peculiar institutions and social usages so long as these were not dangerous to the state. Thus the Jews of the *medinah* formed a practically autonomous community. They had perfect freedom in the practice of their religion. The native laws were administered by a native magistracy—the *Zekenim* (elders, sheikhs) so frequently mentioned in the narrative of the Chronicler—a kind of informal senate, in which lay the germ of the future sanhedrin. The all-important matter for the welfare of the colony was the disposition of its pekhah for the time being. Just as it is in Persia or Turkey at the present time, where the character of shah or sultan is of less consequence to the provincials than that of the local wizir or pasha, so it was in the ancient Persian empire. Darius had fixed the amount of tribute-money to be levied from each province, but—and this was a weak point of his system—not the revenues of his satraps and pekhoth; these had to make their office pay itself, and in most cases they did so by extortion. So long, however, as Darius, their declared patron and protector, reigned at Susa and Zerubbabel, their own countryman, held office at Jerusalem, the Jews were secure against the exactions and petty tyrannies of which they had bitter experience afterwards.

Nothing is known with certainty as to when and for what reason Zerubbabel ceased to be governor of Judea, where and in what manner his life ended. The last representative of the house of David who is anything more than a name, slips away like a shadow from the page of history. The latest reference to him is made by Zechariah, when that Prophet declares that the man who founded the Temple shall have the honour of completing it.[1] But there is no indication that this prophecy was literally fulfilled, and the name of Zerubbabel is significantly absent from the narrative of the dedication of the

---

[1] See *uprà*, p. 170.

Temple. It may be that he never returned from his mission to the court of Darius: if he did return, it was probably only for a time, the tradition being that he spent his closing years and died at Babylon.[1] Either the Jewish prince had fallen under suspicion at court, and was consequently deprived of his office and recalled from Judea;[2] or, finding that his presence at Jerusalem gave a handle to the enemies of his countrymen in their intrigues, patriotically resigned; or, perhaps the best-founded conjecture, threw up his post in despair, weary of the strife of parties and rivalry of ambitions within the community itself. The actual position of Zerubbabel, as a subordinate official of a foreign state, could not but clash with the national sentiment

---

[1] *Seder olam sutta:*—'Zerubbabel, in the first year of Cyrus, went with the exiles to Jerusalem; but returned again to Babylon, and died there.'

[2] 'We are of opinion that Darius, while keeping the promise made by his predecessor to complete the Temple and re-establish the Jewish worship, nevertheless gave so much credence to the fears expressed by the governor of the lands beyond Euphrates as to withdraw from Palestine the members of the royal family, who alone had it in their power to rekindle the ancient ideas of nationality. Darius willingly kept them in Persia, at the head of the Jews who had remained in great numbers in his vast empire.'—Derenbourg, *Hist. de la Palestine*, 20.

THE END OF A DYNASTY. 221

which saw in him the inheritor of a great tradition, the representative of a royal line compared with which those that had risen up on the Euphrates and the Choaspes were mere mushroom growths. No doubt, as years passed on, leaving the dynastic hope unfulfilled, the decided royalist feeling which had at first prevailed among the Bene ha-Golah —to which Haggai had given open, and Zechariah more guarded expression—dwindled down, and a lessening circle of supporters rallied round the heir of the ancient monarchy. For a time, after the accession of Darius, there had been some ground for hoping that Zerubbabel might be permitted to mount the throne of his ancestors. Under Persian rule, the Phœnicians, the Cilicians, and probably other of the subject nations, were allowed to retain their native sovereigns,[1] the Persian satrap at these courts holding a position similar to that of the British Resident at Hyderabad or Baroda. But no such concession was made to Jewish feeling, and even the most sanguine royalist

---

[1] Herod. vii. 98.

might despair of obtaining from any future king what had been withheld by a monarch otherwise so well disposed towards the Jews as the son of Hystaspes. In all probability, the idea of a monarchical restoration had already become distasteful alike to the *Zekenim* or Notables, who looked upon Zerubbabel as only *primus inter pares;* and to the High Priest and his faction, now conscious of growing power. Traces of friction between Prince and Pontiff, between the partisans of the throne and of the altar, are found in at least one poem of that day which seems to have been designed as an eirenicon. The emphatic reference to 'the thrones of the house of David' in connection with 'the house of Jehovah'—the earnest, reiterated appeals for peace in the interests of the newly-restored worship—the solemn adjuration to 'pray for the peace of Jerusalem'[1]—point to a state of matters within the colony which may perhaps account for Zerubbabel's departure. A man of courage and resolution might have grappled successfully with these difficul-

---

[1] Psalm cxxii.

tics. But so far as can be gathered from the scanty notices of his career, Zerubbabel, however well-meaning, seems to have lacked the firmness and address which were needed to hold in check competitors for power, to satisfy the popular sentiment, and at the same time to avoid giving cause for suspicion to the foreign masters of the land.

Of Zerubbabel's numerous posterity,[1] none, so far as is known, succeeded him in office or played a prominent part in national affairs. The Davidic 'legend,' long after it had died out in Judea, lingered on in Babylonia and Persia, where the foreign branch of the line was held in honour as representing the ancient dynasty. At a later date, which cannot be fixed, a certain shadowy sovereignty over the Jews scattered abroad became hereditary in this family, with the title *Resh Galutha*— 'Chief of the Captivity.' The Judean branch sank into comparative obscurity. If any descendant of Zerubbabel at Jerusalem bore the title of *Nasi* or Prince of Judah, it was merely by courtesy; henceforth the people

---

[1] 1 Chron. iii. 19 ff.

sought and found their leaders outside the Davidic family. But there were men among the Judeans who clung to the dynastic hope long after it had been abandoned by the mass of their countrymen—staunch Legitimists, devoted adherents of a sinking or sunken cause. The High Priest and his supporters naturally exulted over the displacement of the man who stood in the way of their supremacy. The populace, which had looked for great things from Zerubbabel, and had been disappointed, bowed to the inevitable, and gave up the dream of a restoration of the monarchy. But the partisans of the throne could not reconcile themselves to this inglorious end of all the glories. Even after their leader had gone or been taken from them, they held by the idea he represented, and would be content with no substitute for the rule of the theocratic king in Israel. This party had its poets, who gave passionate expression to the feeling of disappointment, of betrayal almost, called forth by Zerubbabel's hapless end, and at the same time to the lingering hope that he might yet return to take his rightful place at the head of Jehovah's people. To these singers it seemed a thing inconceivable that Jehovah could have cast off His anointed. For the moment the sceptre was broken and the crown lay in the dust, but the Covenant remained, the indefeasible title to the throne of David and his seed for ever :—

> 'Thou spakest in vision to thy saints,
>   And saidst, I have laid help upon one that is mighty;
>   I have exalted one chosen out of the people.
>   I have found David my servant ;
>   With my holy oil have I anointed him. . . .
>   I also will make him my first-born,
>   The highest of the kings of the earth.
>   My mercy will I keep for him for evermore,
>   And my covenant shall stand fast with him.
>   His seed also will I make to endure for ever,
>   And his throne as the days of heaven. . .
>   My covenant will I not break,
>   Nor alter the thing that is gone out of my lips.
>   Once have I sworn by my holiness ;
>   I will not lie unto David ;
>   His seed shall endure for ever,
>   And his throne as the sun before me.'[1]

Between the promised glory and permanence of the royal house and its present fallen state, there is a strange incongruity, perplexing to the man in whose mind religion

---

[1] Ps. lxxxix. 19-20, 27-29, 34-36.

and loyalty are fused in one master-passion:—

'But thou hast cast off and rejected,
Thou hast been wroth with thine anointed.
Thou hast abhorred the covenant of thy servant:
Thou hast profaned his crown even to the ground. . .
Thou hast exalted the right hand of his adversaries;
Thou hast made all his enemies to rejoice. . . .
How long, O Jehovah, wilt thou hide thyself for ever?
How long shall thy wrath burn like fire?'[1]

Another singer recalls the services rendered by Zerubbabel to the community, his share in the building of the Temple, for which he seems so poorly rewarded:—

'Jehovah, remember for David
All his affliction;
How he sware unto Jehovah,
And vowed unto the Mighty One of Jacob:
Surely I will not come into the tabernacle of my house,
Nor go up into my bed;
I will not give sleep to mine eyes,
Or slumber to mine eyelids;
Until I find out a place for Jehovah,
A tabernacle for the Mighty One of Jacob.'[2]

This poet also lays stress upon the Covenant, and claims for his Prince, as lineal descendant and heir of David, the fulfilment of

---

[1] Ps. lxxxix. 38-39, 42, 46.
[2] Ps. cxxxii. 1-5.

the promise made to the founder of the dynasty :—

> 'For thy servant David's sake
> Turn not away the face of thine anointed.
> Jehovah hath sworn unto David in truth;
> He will not turn from it:
> Of the fruit of thy body will I set upon thy throne.'[1]

The allusions of this writer to the shame which shall cover the 'enemies of David,'[2] and to the righteousness which shall clothe the priesthood of the future,[3] betray the embittered feeling of the royalist partisans against the hierarchy which chiefly profited by Zerubbabel's fall, and whose intrigues perhaps had helped to bring it about. These lyrics of reproach and regret were the only resource of men debarred from action. They might invest with a certain pathos the personality of the banished Prince, and keep him from being absolutely forgotten by his contemporaries. But they could effect nothing against the irresistible forces of the time which doomed the Davidic house to the obscurity of a private station, and made for ever impossible a restoration of the Davidic throne.

---

[1] Ps. cxxxii. 10 11. [2] *Ibid.*, 18. [3] *Ibid.*, 9, 16.

CHAPTER XII.

Joel ben Pethuel.

NEXT to the completion of the Temple, the object that had lain nearest the heart of the Jewish colonists was the rebuilding of the walls of Jerusalem. So long as the city stood unwalled, it was at the mercy of any Arab razzia or hostile incursion of the Samaritans or Idumeans, and now the danger was felt more acutely than ever, for the sanctuary had to be defended. The complaisance of Darius had not gone so far as to permit the fortifying of Jerusalem. The natural strength of the place was itself a reason for refusing the petition of the Jews; their city had a bad record in the matter of sieges; it would be less likely to give trouble wanting its walls. The colonists, baffled hitherto, still hoped to carry their point, and no sooner had Xerxes followed Darius on the throne than they found means to bring their suit before the new sovereign.[1] At once the Samaritan opposition broke out afresh. The 'adversaries' had not been able to do more than delay the building of the Temple; they now exerted themselves to the utmost to prevent the building of the walls. Samaria was a fortified town, the seat of an official who apparently held or claimed higher rank than the Jewish pekhah, and the Samaritans naturally looked with jealous eyes on the establishment of a rival stronghold within one day's journey of their capital. They lost no time in sending to court what the Chronicler calls 'letters of accusation'[2]—in which, perhaps, the Jews were charged with being in league with the Egyptians, now in full revolt against the Persian crown. The matter came before Xerxes on the eve of his invasion of Egypt. The same reasons for favouring the stronger nation at the expense of the weaker which had prevailed in Cambyses' time, prevailed now. The Samaritan letters carried the day, the prayer of

---

[1] Ezra iv. 6.   [2] *Ibid.*

the Jews was rejected, and Jerusalem remained unwalled.

During the re-conquest and chastisement of Egypt, which Xerxes rapidly accomplished in the second year of his reign (484 B.C.), the colonists had to undergo a repetition of the same hardships which they had experienced in the days of Cambyses. Once again the war was brought to their very doors. Their fidelity to the Persians exposed them to the enmity of the insurgent Egyptians, while the robber-bands of Idumea, taking advantage of the unsettled state of these countries, raided at will across their borders. By the prophet of that day, Egypt and Edom are expressly denounced for 'the violence done to the children of Judah, because they have shed innocent blood in their land.'[1] The Jewish colony, lying helpless between the combatants, suffered from both sides. The march of the Persian armies through the land suggested the figure of a plague of locusts, coming up in flight after flight, 'laying waste the vine and barking the fig-tree.'[2] Those were evil days

---

[1] Joel iii. 19.   [2] *Ibid.*, i. 4, 7.

for the Judeans; they probably found their own troubles sufficiently engrossing, and gave little heed to what passed elsewhere. Yet one event of that time had a significance of its own which no pious Israelite could fail to appreciate. It was in the beginning of Xerxes' reign that a great prophecy was fulfilled, and the blow, long suspended, fell upon an ancient enemy. Babylon, which Cyrus had treated so leniently, which even Darius had spared, met with no mercy at the hands of Xerxes, against whom it rose in a last revolt. By that monarch the fanes of Babylon were plundered and destroyed, and the great golden image of Bel was carried off to Susa in triumph. Thus at last 'Bel bowed down and Nebo crouched; their idols were given up to the beasts and to the cattle'[1]—and this was fitted to confirm the faith of Israel in that high Hand which guided its destinies. The heathen shrine where once the sacred vessels of the sanctuary had stood as trophies was now swept away for ever. The temple of Je-

---

[1] Isa. xlvi. 1.

hovah had risen from its ruins; the temple of Bel had fallen.

The Grecian expedition of Xerxes, undertaken on a scale such as the world had never yet witnessed, followed the re-conquest of Babylon. In the list of nations given by Herodotus as composing the vast host which gathered at Sardis in the autumn of 481, the name of the Jews does not appear. Herodotus indeed makes mention of 'the Syrians of Palestine' as furnishing a contingent,[1] but by these he evidently means the Philistines, not the Palestinian Jews. Josephus claims the *Solymi*, referred to by a Greek poet in the same connection, as his countrymen, and on this bases his confident assertion that 'our nation came to the assistance of King Xerxes in his war against Greece;'[2] but in this he is quite mistaken, as the Solymi were an ancient and well-known people of Asia Minor, and *Solyma*, as an abbreviated (Greek) name for Jerusalem (*Hierosolyma*), did not come into use until a much later date. But though

---

[1] Herod., vii. 89.
[2] *Contra Apion.* i. 22., cp. Tacitus, *Hist.* v. 2 :—*Alii Judæorum initia, Solymos, carminibus Homeri celebratam gentem, conditam urbem Hierosolyma nomine suo fecisse.*

the Judeans are not mentioned in the list of nations, for the reason that they were neither numerous nor important, it may be taken as certain that they had their place, however humble, in the mighty armament of the Persian king. No nation or tribe in the empire was exempted from military service, any more than from payment of tribute; and with Xerxes it was a point of honour, a thing on which he prided himself, that every land under his sceptre should send its sons to swell the *grande armée* of antiquity. The memorable issue of that campaign, the names of Thermopylae, Salamis and Plataea, belong not to Jewish but to universal history. It is possible that the allusion of the Hebrew prophet to 'the Northerner,' turning his back on the western sea and coming to a shameful end [1]—may point obscurely to the melting away of the Persian myriads, and the homeward flight of their king, baffled and disgraced.

During the reign of Xerxes, alike in time of peace as of war, the condition of the Jewish

---

[1] Joel ii. 20.

colony became steadily worse. Not even in the dark days before the building of the Temple, not within living memory, had there been such distress in the land.[1] The men who followed Zerubbabel in office were probably for the most part foreigners. There may have been an occasional pekhah of Hebrew race, but it seems to have made little difference to the Judeans whether their governor for the time being was a fellow-countryman or an alien. No man of the type of Zerubbabel—a patriot first, and a Persian official only second—appeared among his successors. The province was handed over to one ruler after another whose sole thought was to live well at the expense of his subjects, and enrich himself by the methods familiar to eastern officialism. In addition to the burden of imperial taxation, the people had to provide 'the bread of the pekhah,' the supplies of that functionary and his household, either in money or in kind, to the amount of forty shekels (about £5) daily.[2] The province might be starving, but the governor and his

---

[1] Joel i. 2. [2] Neh. v. 14, 15.

petty court must live on the fat of the land. Nothing that was not of the best need be offered to the great man; the prophet reproaches his countrymen for bringing blemished animals to the altar: 'present it now unto your pekhah; will *he* be pleased with you?'—he asks sardonically.[1] More galling even than such exactions was the insolence of the pekhah's retainers, the meanest of whom looked down on and oppressed the subject Jews. 'The pekhoth that were before me,' writes Nehemiah, 'laid burdens upon the people .... yea, even their servants lorded it over the people.'[2] All the evils of Asiatic despotism weighed upon the Bene ha-Golah—venal justice, confiscation of property, military conscription enforced by those who had 'power over their bodies.'[3] They were 'in great distress,'[4] and the hardest thing of all to bear was the reflection that this land, in which they were now servants, victims of oppression, and of which the revenues went to a foreign king, was their own land, which

---

[1] Mal. i. 8.
[2] Neh. v. 15. ' . . *exploited* the people' (Reuss). Neh. ix. 37.   [4] *Ibid.*

Jehovah had given to their fathers to possess and enjoy.[1] A writer of a later day, who paints vividly the circumstances of this time in describing his own, indicates the one thought that might console Israel, impatient of indignity and extortion—the thought of that supreme justice and rule to which the mightiest potentate of this world is subject. 'If thou seest the poor man oppressed,' says Koheleth, 'and justice and judgment in robbers' hands in the medinah, marvel not thereat; One higher than the high regardeth, and the highest is over them.' And Koheleth adds the characteristically shrewd reflection that after all the bad might be worse, that despotism is at least better than anarchy :—'And on the whole 'tis of advantage to the land, that a king is over the cultivated field.'[2]

With the few passing words already noticed,[3] the Chronicler dismisses the period covered by the reign of Xerxes (486-465 B.C.), and as his narrative is only resumed with the seventh year of Artaxerxes I., who followed Xerxes on

---

[1] Neh. ix. 36, *cp.* Lament. v. 2.
[2] Eccles. v. 8, 9.   [3] *Suprà*, p. 229.

the throne, there is left a gap in the national annals of more than quarter of a century. The Book of Esther professes to fill up the gap to some extent, by giving an account of certain marvellous events in Jewish history which transpired during the reign of Xerxes. According to that Book, while the Jews at home remained in total obscurity, the Jews abroad were playing a conspicuous part in the affairs of the empire. While the community of the second Temple suffered from a dearth of great men, the Golah had produced both a hero and a heroine. While the Judeans were painfully striving to re-establish the ancient cultus, their countrymen in Persia had originated a new festival, whose popularity was almost to eclipse that of the old. While at Jerusalem the years dragged monotonously on, unmarked by any outstanding event, by any episode that recalled in the slightest degree the ancient marvels of Jewish history, at Susa there had been a terrible danger and a wonderful, divine deliverance of the chosen people.

This Book of Esther, if it were possible to take it as an authentic narrative of real events, composed in the vein of sober history at a time not too far removed from that when the events took place, would have considerable value as throwing light upon the fortunes of the Jews abroad and their position under the Persian empire, at a most interesting period otherwise barren of all record. But even if the Book were historical, and not merely a late recoction of a popular legend, with how much or how little basis of fact it is impossible to say—it might be set aside without any loss to the history of the Jews of Judea. The writer of the Book of Esther does not once refer to the holy land or the holy city—an omission scarcely less surprising than that of the holy Name. So far as he is concerned, the Return might never have taken place, the Temple never have been rebuilt. His hero Mordecai, the Hebrew patriot, the all-powerful vizier of the Gentile king, does not lift a finger to help the colony of his countrymen, painfully struggling to establish themselves on Jewish soil. However it may have been with the Golah in Xerxes' day, the Judeans seem neither to have suffered specially under Haman nor benefited under Mordecai.

There is, however, one Book—prophetical,

not historical—which touches on certain salient features of Jewish social and political life at this period. Joel ben Pethuel does not, like Haggai and Zechariah, date his prophecies by the years of the Great King, but there is strong internal evidence that he wrote in the time of Xerxes, and was thus the penultimate prophet of Judah. His Book contains not a scrap of autobiography, not a stroke of conscious self-portraiture; possibly, like Zechariah, he may have been a member of the priesthood, but even that does not necessarily follow from his frequent and sympathetic references to the Temple, its ritual and its hierarchy. Joel is not at all a prophet of action, a personage in public life, after the manner of Zechariah; he is a thinker and writer, rather than an orator and statesman. In style and diction he is singularly free from any mark of a period of literary decadence. The drapery of the ideas, sometimes the ideas themselves, suggest a close study of the ancient prophetic books, the classics of the nation; his work shows signs of the scholar's lamp as well as of the sacred fire. But there is a native vigour and independence in this writer, a force and freedom of thought and expression, which lift his work distinctly above the level of Jewish post-exile literature.

The picture which Joel presents of the state of matters in Judea is doleful in the extreme. Scarcely a gleam of light flickers across the darkness of his page, and even when he gives expression to a hope of better things, it is with reference to a far-off future time, the signs of whose coming are apparent only to a prophet's eye. Among the causes of the national distress was the cycle of bad seasons, which still lasted as in the days of Haggai and Zechariah. A great drought parched the fields. The granaries were empty, the corn-seed shrivelled under the clods, the vintage and olive-crop failed, the cattle lowed piteously in the withered pastures, there was dearth in the land.[1] The hostility of the neighbouring peoples added to the sufferings of the colonists. They lay at the mercy of their enemies, too weak to defend themselves, too poor to buy the protection of the Persian authorities. They had neither walls nor military force to prevent 'strangers

---

[1] Joel i. 10, 17-20.

passing through Jerusalem.'[1] Phœnicians as well as Edomites harried Jewish territory, and plundered Jewish towns.[2] Jewish captives passed into the hands 'of the slave-dealers of Tyre and Sidon, who carried on a brisk trade in this kind of merchandise with the Greeks; and nothing so much excites the prophet's indignation, his longing for the day of judgment on the Gentiles, as the thought of the hapless fate of these children of Judah, torn from their homes and sold into bondage and shame.[3]

Among the results of the prevailing distress was one which afflicted the pious Israelite more poignantly than any personal damage or loss. By the decree of King Darius, the costs of the daily oblation had been charged on the revenues of the Syrian province,[4] but this arrangement seems to have lapsed during the reign of Xerxes, who had no special favour for the Jews, and whose officials naturally took their cue from their sovereign. If this, the central act of the national worship, was to be continued, it must be by a voluntary assessment of the people themselves, a means which

---

[1] Joel iii. 17.
[2] *Ibid.*, 4, 5.
[3] *Ibid.*, 3, 6-8.
[4] *Supra*, p. 186.

may possibly have been tried for a time, until the burden became too heavy for the poverty-stricken community, and at last the service of the altar completely failed. This collapse of the ritual within forty years after the restoration of the Temple seems to Joel the very climax of calamity. The daily offering typified the ideal relation, the continuous intercourse between Jehovah and His people; it was the pledge of divine blessing unfailingly renewed, so long as the people kept alive the fire of Jehovah on His altar and the faith of Jehovah in their hearts. With the lapse of this observance, it seemed as though the intercourse were suspended, the covenant relation broken, the pledge of blessing forfeited, and Israel abandoned by its God. Again and again the prophet laments that 'the meal offering and the drink offering is cut off from the house of Jehovah.'[1] It is of all signs of the times that which fills him with gloomiest forebodings. It forbids any thought of joy or hope of prosperity. It seems the evident precursor of the approaching end of all things.

---

[1] Joel i. 9, 13, 16; ii. 14.

The cessation of the daily offering is not charged by Joel as a fault against either priesthood or people. He recognises it as resulting from their want of means, not their want of will, that they have failed to pay their dues to Jehovah's altar. Indeed, the writings of this prophet throughout, though almost uniformly cheerless, are singularly free from the accent of blame. He has no occasion to denounce any tendency to idolatry, which had been the staple theme of the great prophets before and during the exile, but of which the exile had made an end. He has not, like Haggai, to reproach his countrymen for paying selfish heed to their own interests and neglecting their religious duties. He does not, like Zechariah, inveigh against those petty vices of fraud and greed which had disfigured the social life of Judea in that prophet's day. There was no outstanding national sin, no lapse into infidelity, which might account for the misfortunes of the Judeans, plunged into poverty, and ground to the dust under Gentile oppression. Their lot seemed to call for pity, rather than rebuke. Why Jehovah should have seemingly cast off His people and 'given

His heritage to reproach,' is to the prophet an enigma. He can find no answer to the question—'Wherefore should they say among the Gentiles, Where is their God?'[1]

The course which Joel recommends in view of this calamitous state of affairs, his sole practical suggestion, is quite in keeping with the spirit of his time. The essentially joyous character of Jewish religion had been necessarily modified under the depressing influence of the evil days on which the nation had fallen. The feast, which formerly had been the great act of worship, was now felt to be less appropriate than the fast as an expression of the religious feeling of Israel. The institution of national fasts, which had grown up during the Captivity, which the returning exiles had brought back with them to their native land, still kept its hold on popular favour; there was as yet no sign of the change predicted by Zechariah, when the days of fasting were to become 'to the house of Judah joy and gladness, and cheerful feasts.'[2] Joel calls upon the priests and elders to proclaim a

---

[1] Joel ii. 17.   [2] Zech. viii. 19.

national fast and convoke a national assembly, by which means the divine pity might be re-awakened and the divine blessing regained. He is too truly a prophet to put any value on an outward observance which is not animated by an inward spirit of devotion, and emphatically bids the people 'rend their heart, and not [merely] their garments.'[1] But he is a prophet of his day as well as of all time, and manifestly attaches no little importance to this proposed act of national self-humiliation, of which he sketches the programme in some detail. The priests, girt with sackcloth, are to take their stand between the porch and altar of the Temple, and to join in loud lamentations and prayers.[2] The elders and populace are to gather to the house of Jehovah with weeping and mourning;[3] none must be absent—not even the newly-wed bridegroom and bride, not even the children of tenderest years.[4] 'Who knows,' says the prophet, 'whether Jehovah will not turn and repent, and leave a blessing behind Him?'[5]

---

[1] Joel ii. 13.
[2] *Ibid.*, i. 13, ii. 17.
[3] *Ibid.*, i. 14, ii. 12.
[4] *Ibid.*, ii. 16.
[5] *Ibid.*, 14.

Joel sums up his prophecy with a promise that this divine blessing shall be bestowed, and with a lurid picture of those 'last times' in which divine judgment shall be executed on the Gentiles. Though now there was famine in the land, the future would bring abundance of corn, wine, and oil; the early and the latter rain would descend upon the parched fields, and the floors would be full of wheat; the children of Zion, who now mourned and fasted, would be glad and rejoice in their God.[1] Amid the awful cataclysm which is about to overtake the Gentile world, Jerusalem shall be the one place of safety, and its children, gathered thither from all the regions where they are now scattered, shall find deliverance there.[2] Against the heathen who have dispossessed Judah of its heritage, and made it the sport of their tyranny, Joel breathes vengeance and slaughter. Reversing the pacific utterance of an earlier seer, he calls for the ploughshares to be beaten into swords, and the pruning-hooks into spears.[3] He exults in the near coming of that 'day of Jehovah,'

---

[1] Joel ii. 19-24.   [2] *Ibid.*, 32.   [3] Joel iii. 10.

when in the Valley of Judgment the secular wrongs of his nation shall be righted, and the fullest measure of retribution dealt out to its oppressors.[1]

The influence of this prophet on the mind of his contemporaries does not seem to have been very marked. A devout minority may have found consolation in his pictures of a brighter future, and his assurances of the ultimate triumph of Israel over all its foes. But the mass of the people, crushed under the weight of present misfortunes, were in no mood to take comfort from the unfolding of a prospect so visionary and remote. The expectations encouraged by the prophets had been again and again disappointed; and among the men who had come out of captivity with such high-set hopes which had been so rudely dashed, prophecy was to a certain extent discredited. If Joel's trumpet-blast[2] woke an echo in the hearts of his countrymen, the echo must soon have died away. They sorely needed a spiritual guide, but the time was passing or past when that spiritual guide could be found

---

[1] Joel iii. 12-17.   [2] Joel ii. 1, 15.

in any prophet. The old order—of which, strictly speaking, Joel is the last representative, for the one prophet who comes after him is a prophet *sui generis*—must give way to the new; the work must pass into other hands. Already, while Joel was delivering his message in Judea with apparently little result, far off the forces were being prepared which, once set in motion, were to take the place of prophetism as the chief factor in the religious life of Israel.

CHAPTER XIII.

The House of Zadok.

SO hopeless seemed the outlook of the Jewish colony in those days that its chiefs felt themselves constrained to do something, to take some new and decisive step, in order to avert the threatened loss of all that had been gained by the Return, sixty years before. The result of the policy initiated by the men of the Return, and adhered to ever since, had been to leave the Judeans isolated, friendless, and at the same time too weak to make themselves feared or respected. After all those years, instead of growing in prosperity, they could just manage to exist in their own land, and no more. The Persian authorities neglected or oppressed them; the neighbouring peoples, whose offers of amity they had repelled, hated and harassed them; their countrymen in Babylonia and Persia had apparently forgotten their existence. It seemed to the leaders of Jewish society that, unless a change of policy were now attempted, the colony must go to pieces and the national enterprise end in ruin.

The authorities in Judea—the native authorities, that is, for the external administration was entirely in foreign hands—were, since the removal or departure of Zerubbabel, the Zekenim or Notables, and the Zadokites headed by the High Priest. These formed two aristocracies—one lay, the other sacerdotal. To them the people looked for rule and guidance in all matters affecting them as Jews, not as subjects of the Persian empire.

The High Priest was now the most prominent figure in the community. His position was not yet recognised by the Persian government, his jurisdiction did not and could not clash with that of the Persian officials; and this gave the representative of the house of Zadok an immense advantage over his rival of the house of David—the tiara might be worn with safety while the crown was impossible. It was almost inevitable that whatever measure of homerule was left to the Judeans by their foreign masters should ultimately centre itself in the hands of the High Priest, whose title and office had come down from a remote antiquity; and the more consciously the people realised that they were in truth a religious sect, without any independent political existence, the more necessary and influential did the pontificate become. Private ambitions and party intrigues may have helped to bring about the supremacy of the High Priest, but, apart from these altogether, that supremacy was in the nature of things. It was, however, slowly, step by step, that the head of the hierarchy rose to be head of the state. In the early days of the Return the power of the pontificate is strictly limited; even when a question arises affecting the rights of the priesthood, it is the temporal ruler of the community, not the spiritual, to whom it is referred and who gives the decision.[1] Haggai alludes to the High Priest throughout as holding a position secondary to that of the Prince. Zechariah does indeed set the crown on his head, but evidently without suspecting the full scope of that symbolic action. Joel

---

[1] Neh. vii. 65.

mentions neither prince nor pontiff, but only the Zekenim or Elders. By the effacement of Zerubbabel the way was cleared for the rise of the High Priest to sovereign power; but it would be a mistake to suppose that either Joshua or any of his successors during the Persian period stepped into the place which the Davidic prince had held in popular estimation. They wanted the Urim and Thummim, and consequently could not claim to give an infallible decision on questions of state. They were not, so far as it appears, consecrated to their office by anointing, as the Law prescribed and as the kings had been consecrated, but simply by investiture.[1] During the century that followed the Return, the High Priest, even in the eyes of his own countrymen, had no sovereign authority. Indeed, there were times when he was not even the first personage in the land.

If the High Priest of those times had any influence beyond his legitimate sphere as representative of the Church, he owed it mainly to his position as head of a powerful caste, the

---

[1] Baudissin, *Priesterthum*, 140.

priestly-patrician houses of Jerusalem. Joshua ben Jehozadak himself seems to have been a man without much force of character; his son Joiakim and his grandson Eliashib who succeeded him were personally little more than ciphers; but they had the hereditary office and title, and at their back stood the great families of their kinsmen, the Bene Zadok, the 'princes of the house of God,' as the Chronicler styles them.[1] These great families, about a score in number, represented the learning and culture, and in a great measure the wealth of Judea, and were naturally looked up to by the people as well as by the lower ranks of the clergy. The Zadokites were by no means free from the egoism of aristocracy. They were quite ready, when occasion served, to convert their social influence into political power, and to use it rather in the interests of their order than for the honour of their religion or the true welfare of the people as a whole.

The pressure of the times told less severely on the Jewish nobility than on the humbler ranks of society. Their greater resources had

---

[1] 1 Chron. ix. 11.

kept them from feeling the actual pinch of want. Still, they could not remain indifferent to the miserable condition of the colony. As a privileged class, they needed for the enjoyment of their privileges a community of prosperous citizens, not a herd of paupers and slaves ; and from them came the impulse which sent the whole people into new paths, the end of which none foresaw. It appeared to the spiritual guides of the nation that a large part of all their troubles might be traced to the attitude taken up by the founders of the colony towards the Amme ha-Aretz, the ' peoples of the land.' Instead of cultivating friendly relations with these peoples, the men of the Return had stiffly refused to hold any intercourse with them or to grant them any share in the religious privileges of Israel. The history of the last sixty years seemed to show that this policy had been a mistake. The founders of the colony had striven to raise a moral barrier betwixt the Gentiles and the Jews, without having the power to raise any physical barrier which alone could keep their enemies at a distance ; and the Gentiles, provoked by their repulse, and by the arrogance of this feeble community which presumed to look down on all other peoples from an eminence of its own, had thwarted and injured them ever since. The colony had never been left in peace, and consequently had never prospered. There was one means of gaining peace that had not yet been tried—to give up these high-flown notions of exclusiveness, to offer now to the Gentiles the comity they had formerly sued for in vain, and to cement that comity by a system of family alliances, from which more friendly relations between the Judeans and their neighbours might reasonably be expected to follow.

It is expressly stated in the memoirs of Ezra that the 'princes and rulers' were the first to contract these marriages with foreigners, and that the common people followed their lead.[1] Evidently the new departure was made deliberately, not merely by individuals on their own responsibility, but as a settled line of policy approved of by the highest authorities in the land. A measure of such startling novelty, so utterly subversive of the principles on which the national life had hitherto been

---

[1] Ezra ix. 2.

based, can scarcely have been resolved upon without serious debate in the quite informal senate or sanhedrin of those days, composed of the chiefs of the priesthood and laity. A majority of these gave their voice for the proposed change, but there was an opposing minority of distinguished laymen [1] who entered their protest against it, and refused to take part in a course of action which they looked upon as criminal. For the present they could do no more than protest. In a matter of this kind, which raised questions of religion as well as of state, the opinion of the High Priest and his kinsmen naturally prevailed; and it does not seem to have occurred to the heads of the hierarchy that, in sanctioning these marriages of Jews with aliens, they were either breaking the Law or violating ancient precedent. Their opponents might quote against them the prohibition addressed to Israel at the time of the conquest of the land, when the people were forbidden to espouse the daughters of the Canaanites under threat of divine vengeance if they disobeyed.[2] But to this it

---

[1] Ezra ix. 1   [2] Deut. vii. 1-5.

might be answered that the times of the Conquest were entirely different from those of the Return; that this article of the Mosaic code had a limited reference, and had never been understood as vetoing all marriages of Jews with Gentiles for all time; that the expressly stated reason for the prohibition, the danger that such unions might lead to idolatry, no longer existed. If the neighbouring peoples had been idolaters like the Canaanites of old, the proposal to intermarry with them would probably never have been made; in any case, the High Priest and his colleagues would not have dared to give their countenance to such a scandal. Undoubtedly the strongest point in favour of the new policy was this, that these peoples were not idolaters, at least did not wish to continue so, but sought an entrance into the Jewish church. At this stage of their history, as often before and since, it was shown to the Jewish people where lay the true secret of their power. Weak in numbers and in material resources, robbed of their liberties, impotent even for self-defence, they were feared by the very enemies who trampled on them, and respected by those who insulted them. There were obvious reasons for the Jews seeking the alliance of the Gentiles, material advantages to be gained; but quite other motives must have actuated the Gentiles in courting alliance with the Jews. The one possession of Israel which seemed enviable to other nations was its religion; ignorantly, but not insincerely, these Amme ha-Aretz desired to share in the religious privileges of the chosen people; the object of their ambition was to have an access to the temple, a 'portion and right in Jerusalem.'[1] The Samaritans already professed themselves worshippers of Jehovah, and among the other nations also there must have been something of that vague discontent with their native idolatries, that dim appreciation of the nobler creed of Israel, which alone could explain their desire to draw closer to a people whose friendship was in all other respects valueless, and whose enmity they could afford to despise. Thus the chiefs of the colony, in embarking on their present course, might argue that they were allying themselves, not with heathens, but with proselytes of the gate;

---

[1] Neh. ii. 20.

and on this ground might claim the support of a party which had not been used to act in concert with the priesthood. The prophets and their following had never been in sympathy with that spirit of exclusiveness which had grown up during the Exile, and which had reigned at the time of the Return. They had rebuked the Jewish pride of race which saw in every alien a perpetual outcast from the commonwealth, and in the worship of Jehovah a spiritual monopoly which must be guarded with jealous care against all intrusion of the Gentiles. The great Prophet of the Exile had spoken a word on the subject of proselytism which could never be forgotten by those who had felt his mighty influence. The foreigner who had 'joined himself to Jehovah' was not to fear lest he might be separated from Jehovah's people; he too should be brought to the 'holy mountain' and 'made joyful in the house of prayer,' for 'Jehovah's house should be called a house of prayer for all peoples'[1]— a conception widely different from that held by the men who drew up the Roll of the

---

[1] Isa. lvi. 3, 6, 7.

Congregation, and built the second Temple. Those who still cherished the prophetic ideal were naturally inclined to look not unfavourably on a measure which presented itself under the specious guise of conceding their just rights to the Gentiles, and widening the way of access into that spiritual commonwealth which was ultimately to comprehend all the nations of the earth. For once, the practical men and the dreamers were at one.

There could be no scruple on the part of the community in following where the family of the High Priest himself showed the way. Priests, Levites, nobles, sought foreign brides; and the common people did as their leaders, all the more readily, it has been suggested,[1] because in the Jewish colony, as in such settlements generally, women were probably few in proportion. Samaritans, Moabites, Ammonites, Egyptians, Philistines, are mentioned among the peoples whose daughters were mated with Judeans.[2] At first the new policy seemed justified by its results. It brought about more friendly relations between the Jews and their

---

[1] Reuss, *Chron. ecclés.*, 219. [2] Ezra ix. 1; Neh. xiii. 23, 28.

neighbours, and in particular laid to rest for a time the old feud with the Samaritans, which had been a source of endless trouble since the morrow of the Return. But this *rapprochement* with the Gentiles, while to some extent smoothing away the external difficulties of the colony, proved in course of years anything but an unmixed good. The Jewish leaders had made the mistake of studying and solving their problem as politicians pure and simple, without giving due heed to the unique position of Israel among the nations, and to the duties and responsibilities which that position involved. If Israel was to fulfil its high mission to the Gentile world, it must still, at this stage of its development, keep separate from the Gentile world. The foundation for the splendid superstructure of prophecy was not yet solidly laid. The time had not come for breaking down the fence and admitting the Gentiles wholesale into the fold of the covenant; Israel was still too unsteady in itself to hold a middle course between isolation and Gentilisation. By abating their claim to be in a religious sense *the* people, by consenting to forego their mission, it might be possible for the Jews to live quietly and even to prosper among the group of petty pashaliks and vassal kingdoms of which, under Persian rule, they formed one; but at that price the benefits of order and security were too dearly bought. The men of the Return had realised this; and their elaborate precautions to secure absolute purity of race in all who joined the colony, though carried to an extreme, were yet essentially sound. The evils which they had apprehended from any other line of policy followed now. A closer contact with the Gentiles distinctly lowered the tone of Jewish religious life. Foreign wives brought with them into Jewish families foreign ways and foreign speech, and the sentiment of nationality, which had formerly been so strong with the Bene ha-Golah, began to give way, sapped by these influences from without. The Law, laxly construed at one point, was infringed or evaded at others. Hitherto an effort had been made, with indifferent success but with honest intention, to revive the ancient institutions of Mosaism; this effort was now abandoned, and actual retrogression followed. In the worship of the Temple, in the ministry of the altar, in the observance of the Sabbath, there was manifested a spirit of carelessness and irreverence which contrasted strongly with the pious fervour of the generation that came out of exile. There was this excuse for the laity, that they knew comparatively little about the Law and its requirements; but none for the priesthood, which made no attempt to enlighten the popular ignorance. Malachi's fiery polemic against the priesthood of Jerusalem belongs to a later day, but the faults with which he charges them—their insincerity, their selfishness, their sacrilegious neglect of the altar—may be traced to the time following the Gentile alliance. The lukewarmness of the hierarchy spread downwards through all grades of Jewish society; and never, even in the darkest hour of the colony, had the horizon been so overcast as now, when there was more of material wellbeing and less of patriotic feeling and religious zeal. The Captivity had been preceded by the age of idolatry; it was being followed by the age of indifference and ignorance. There was still in Israel that sound core of religious life which had never been wanting even in the worst period of national infidelity. There were still those who 'trembled at the name of Jehovah,' and who looked with shame and sorrow on the degeneracy of their countrymen. But these faithful few could do little or nothing to arouse a people sunk in spiritual lethargy; the forces against them were too strong. It was scarcely possible to hope that the Reformer whom the age needed could spring from native soil. To cope with indifference and ignorance, he must be at once a zealot and a teacher. To measure himself successfully against the ruling classes of Judea, he must be clad with an authority higher than theirs. The Reformer must come from without, if at all—from Babylon, from the midst of that greater Israel which still dwelt among the Gentiles. From the North, whence formerly had come the destroyer, the saviour of society must come.

CHAPTER XIV.

The Israel Abroad.

WHILE these changes were taking place in Judea, the community of the foreign Jews had likewise been passing through a process of transition, and in this, the second generation after the Return, the results of forces which had long been working silently under the surface came forth to view. Starting from the same point, and under the pressure of circumstances in some respects similar, the Israel abroad had developed itself in a direction exactly opposite to that taken by the Israel at home. The Judeans, finding themselves encircled by idolatrous or semi-idolatrous populations which refused to let them go their own way in quiet, and offered them the alternative of alliance or open enmity, had chosen the former, and deliberately taken a course which tended to obliterate or at least obscure the distinctions between Jew and Gentile. The Babylonian and Persian Jews also found themselves in closest touch externally with the heathen; but this very proximity, instead of tempting them to coalesce with the native populations of the lands in which they dwelt, only bound them the more strictly together, and confirmed them in the attitude of unswerving resistance to all Gentile influences and advances.

From one point of view the foreign Jews were apparently at a disadvantage as compared with their brethren of the medinah. These had Jerusalem, the temple, the priestly organisation, the ritual system; and formed, at least nominally, a separate people occupying its own territory. The Golah, on the other hand, had no political centre and rallying-point, no material basis for its national life, no outward props to lean upon. But for this very reason it clung all the more tenaciously to those spiritual possessions which alone gave it a title to existence, and for the defence of which it had to make a conscious, continuous effort. Thus what seemed the loss of the Golah proved actually its gain. Israel of the Province had its geographical frontier-line, which was more of a semblance than a reality, but had the effect of making other safeguards seem less necessary. Israel of the Empire had nothing to depend on but its moral frontier-line, which it valued all the more on that account, and which, faithfully maintained, proved more effective than rivers or deserts.

Thus it came to pass with these two bodies of the same people that a similar environment produced quite opposite tendencies—in the case of the Judeans, increasing laxity; in the case of the foreign Jews, increasing strictness of doctrine and practice. The points at which the Judeans had yielded were precisely those at which the Golah made its firmest stand. At Jerusalem it was now considered lawful to wed a daughter of the Gentiles. In Babylon, among the Jews who kept true to their religion and nationality, such a thing was unheard of; a man must 'take a wife of the seed of his fathers,' and not a 'strange woman,'[1] otherwise he was looked on as a recreant Israelite who had polluted the 'holy

---

[1] Tobit iv. 12.

seed.'[1] At Jerusalem the Hebrew language was passing into disuse, giving way to foreign jargons brought in by foreigners;[2] in Babylon, it was cherished as the sacred speech in which the divine revelation had been given, in which the finest thoughts of the highest minds of Israel were preserved; even while using Aramaic in their necessary intercourse with the Gentiles, the Jews were careful to keep alive the knowledge of their native language among themselves. At Jerusalem the Sabbath was still kept in the primitive fashion, men 'doing their pleasure'[3] on that day without any idea of its special sanctity; but in Babylonia this ancient popular institution had assumed a new spiritual character, and was observed most strictly, no longer with the gaiety of a festival, but as a solemn day of rest and prayer. The Jewish Sabbath, properly so called, may be said to have originated in Babylon. Its importance as an outward symbol of Judaism, a 'sign of the covenant,'[4] had been recognised at an early period of the Captivity, and had grown in the

---

[1] Ezra ix. 2.
[2] Neh. xiii. 24.
[3] Isa. lviii. 13.
[4] Ezek. xx. 12, 20.

course of years. Already Ezekiel speaks of 'keeping' the feasts, but of 'hallowing' the Sabbath;[1] and the great Exile-Prophet, who as a rule lays slight stress on points of ceremonial, exclaims, 'Blessed is the man who keepeth the Sabbath from profaning it!'[2] Of all the institutions of Mosaism none was better fitted than this to quicken and sustain the national consciousness of Israel in exile. Each seventh day as it came round reminded the Jew most forcibly that he was a Jew, marked him out visibly from the mass of surrounding heathenism, and strengthened the bond of union with his co-religionists and compatriots, whom the day of rest brought together for those simple rites of devotion which alone were possible on foreign soil. To the Jews abroad the Sabbath was 'the holy thing of Jehovah,'[3] long before any such view found acceptance with the Jews at home.

In other respects the situation of the Babylonian Jews was more favourable to the evolution of their religious-national life than that of the Palestinians. Dispersed over the provinces

---

[1] Ezek. xliv. 24.   [2] Isa. lvi. 2.   [3] Isa. lviii. 13.

of the empire, apparently disunited, yet knit together by the indissoluble ties of religion and custom, the Jewish communities in Persia and Babylonia were freed from political anxieties, and were spared that struggle for existence which absorbed the energies of the colonists of Jerusalem. No strife of parties within, no violent aggressions from without, troubled or hindered the peaceable course of their spiritual development. Living more immediately under the sceptre of the Great King, in the rich central provinces of the monarchy, they suffered less from the evils of oriental despotism than the Judeans in their remote and ill-governed pashalik. And the high culture and civilisation of these lands was not without its influence on Jewish thought and manners —an influence essentially of a negative kind, but none the less very powerful. The Golah could produce a type which was impossible in such a state of society as that existing at Jerusalem. It produced men of learning, of polish and refinement, of broad views and great experience in affairs; men who had amassed riches and risen to high station among the Gentiles, without in any way proving false to the traditions of their race. A Jew of this type, going up from Babylon or Susa to Jerusalem, while he felt that he was visiting the holy city of his people, could not but feel also that he had left the metropolis of the world, the middle point of culture and power, for an obscure outlying province which seemed by comparison only semi-civilised.

Intellectually as well as spiritually the Jews had profited by their expatriation. The marvellous literary fecundity of the period of the Exile may be attributed, in part at least, to the influence of foreign culture on the Jewish mind, as well as to that detachment from other pursuits which was a necessary consequence of their situation as a people without a polity. This period had left to the nation a magnificent legacy — master-pieces in history, in poetry, in philosophy, which showed the genius of the race at its highest and finest. Still, half-a-century and more after the Return, the literary activity, combined with the intensity of religious feeling, survived; but its character and direction had undergone a change. Prophetism had departed with the emigrants from Babylon: its last efforts in the field of action were put forth on Jewish soil. The Golah was no longer under the living influence of prophecy; its literary activity ceased to be creative, original; the tendency now was to go back upon the old paths rather than to strike boldly forth into new. The problem which the leaders of Israel *in partibus infidelium* had continually before them, was how best to conserve Jewish nationality on the basis of Jewish religion. On the solving of this problem were concentrated all the energies of powerful minds, spurred on by the necessities of a situation which brought home to them at every turn the dangers that menaced the people, cut loose from its ancient moorings and cast adrift on a pagan world. What they sought, what Israel needed, was a force at once of cohesion and repulsion, by which this scattered people might be made to feel its essential unity, and enabled to withstand the assaults or insidious approaches of heathendom. Prophecy could not supply this force. Prophecy had given to Israel its highest spiritual and ethical ideas; had kindled the Messianic hope; had conjured forth the enthusiasm which led first to the Return and afterwards to the building of the

Temple. But what the people needed now was a principle of guidance and control which should appeal to them, not at the rarer moments of spiritual exaltation, but at every hour of the common day; which should cover the whole field of social and domestic life, and bear directly on all its duties and relations. They found this in that great body of doctrine and tradition which had grown with the nation's growth, and which now, under the title *Torah Mosheh*,[1] 'Teaching of Moses,' began to assert a supremacy no longer episodic and partial as heretofore, but permanent and absolute. The heroic age of Israel was over. Its leaders now were mere mediocrities in comparison with those mighty figures of the past which had towered in majesty above the common level of men, and stamped on the whole nation the impress of their personality. But the work which warriors had striven to accomplish by the power of the sword, and prophets by the power of abstract ideas—the work of welding

---

[1] The word *Torah*—from a verb-stem meaning *to throw out* (as *the hand* in teaching); hence *to point out, indicate*—signifies *doctrine, instruction*. This wider meaning of the word is lost in the usual translation by νόμος, *Law*.

the people into one compact whole, was now being accomplished, unobtrusively yet steadily and surely, by the power of a Book, the Book of the Law. To this the people turned as to the very 'fountain of wisdom,' 'the book of the commandments of God,' the imperishable Torah, which to keep was life, and to forsake destruction.[1] In this they found the firm standing-ground, the sure weapon and the armour of proof which exiled Israel needed in its perpetual conflict with a heathen world. Not every man could scale the sublime heights and breathe the rarefied air of prophecy; but any might tread the lowlier path of scrupulous obedience to the Law. The Torah of Moses supplanted the Toroth of the Prophets.

Partly as a cause, partly as a consequence of this zeal for the Law, there rose among the Golah a new order, or rather a new development of an old order — the *sopherim*[2] or

---

[1] Baruch iii. 12; iv. 1.

[2] *Sopher* is from *Sepher*, *a book*, and that from the verb-stem meaning *to scrape, to smoothe*—hence, to prepare the skin of an animal for purposes of writing. The Talmudic derivation of *Sopher*—from the verb-stem meaning *to count*, because, it is said, the scribes of old *counted* all the letters of the Law—is purely imaginative.

scribes, who play so great a part in th
history of Judaism. The sopherim were
originally the *penmen* of the community,
masters of the rare art of writing—secretaries
at court, draughtsmen of royal edicts, keepers
of the army muster-rolls. The name was given
to those also who made copies of the prophetic
and other sacred writings, and who did not
always restrict themselves to the copyist's
function, for Jeremiah has occasion to denounce
the 'lying stylus of the sopherim.'[1] The
period of the Exile brought the savants, the
literary experts, into prominence, and gave a
new impulse and aim to their activity. Theirs
was the task of retrieving the national literature
from the wreck of the national fortunes. They
copied, commented, re-cast, wrote; their
scholarship kept the language from falling
into disuse and decay; their diligent research
was largely instrumental in saving the people
from the worst of all possible calamities—from
ignorance of its own past. In course of time
their activity, which had ranged over the
whole field of Jewish historical literature,

---

[1] Jer. viii. 8.

became focussed on the Torah of Moses, the Book of the Law. The sopherim of the Captivity were drawn mainly from the ranks of the priesthood.[1] So far as the priestly office was connected with the sacrificial system, it had necessarily lapsed on foreign soil; but there was one great function of the priesthood which might still be exercised even in the land of exile. They had not the altar, but they had the Book. They could not sacrifice, but they could teach. This function, which Ezekiel had expressly assigned to the Zadokites of Jerusalem,[2] and which they had shamefully neglected, was now taken up most zealously by the sons of Aaron among the Golah. Among the sopherim were the *mebinim*[3]— *teachers* of the people. From the first, they had realised the importance of this duty. Ezekiel, who is scribe as well as prophet, gathers the heads of the people around him, and instructs them in the difference between

---

[1] Wellhausen, *Pharisäer und Sadducäer*, 13.

[2] 'They (the Bene Zadok) shall teach my people the difference between the sacred and the profane:' Ezek. xliv. 23. Cp. Mal. ii. 7—'For the priest's lips should keep knowledge, and they should seek the Law at his mouth.'

[3] Ezra viii. 16; Neh. viii. 7, 9.

things clean and unclean.[1] Among the maxims attributed to Ezra is this — *Teach; make many disciples.* Filled with the conviction that ignorance was impiety, the sopherim laboured to multiply their disciples, and to extend that knowledge without which holiness of life was unattainable. Those popular assemblies which the Sabbaths and holy days brought together gave them the opportunity of making known the Law, and at the same time of expounding it in their own sense, to an ever-widening circle of their countrymen. Once the prophetic word had thrilled those Jewish conventicles, now they hung upon the voice of the scribe, as he read from his roll of the Torah, and exhorted to obedience.

At first the study of the sacred records was carried on by scholars working independently, each on his own lines. But community of pursuits and identity of aim gradually drew these labourers together; the sopherim came to be recognised as a distinct guild or corporation in the community.[2] At Babylon the Jews had under their eyes a striking illustra-

---

[1] Ezek. xxii. 26.   [2] 1 Chron. ii. 55.   *Cp.* 1 Macc. vii. 12.

tion of what might be done by a class of learned men for the literature and education of a people—they knew how much the famed 'wisdom of Babylon' was owing to the continuous labour of the Kasdim, that unique order whose store of learning had been handed down from immemorial time by generation after generation of scholars. But apart from any foreign example, the formation of a guild of sopherim was in keeping both with the precedents of the past and with the tendencies of the present. Instances of men binding themselves together for religious objects were furnished by the Levites of old and by the 'colleges of the prophets;' while the lists in the Books of Ezra and Nehemiah abundantly testify how much in vogue such combinations were among the Jews of post-exilian times.[1] United in this fashion, the sopherim did a work and exercised an influence which would have been impossible otherwise. They had their tradition of scholarship, their canons of exegesis, their common stock of results to which many minds had contributed. They

[1] Wellhausen, *Phar. u. Sadd.*, 11.

stood high in the respect of the people as authorities on points of dogma and arbiters in matters of conduct. The people necessarily had to take the Law as their teachers gave it; the sopherim were the intermediaries in doctrine, as the priests were in sacrifice. In striving to establish the supremacy of the Law, they made themselves, as its interpreters, a power to be reckoned with henceforth in Israel. A natural interaction set in—the men exalted the Book: the Book exalted the men. The first stage of sopherism was to explore the Law; the second, to make it 'understanded of the people;' from that, the transition to the third was easy—to make it not only understood but obeyed. The scholar became a teacher, the teacher became a master. 'Let it be done according to the Law,' was their formula.[1] With this Book in their hands, represented as the very word and will of the Eternal, revealed to the first and greatest of the prophets, and by him communicated to the chosen people as the perfect,

---

[1] Ezra x. 3.

infallible code, applicable to all concerns of life, public and private, civil and ecclesiastical — the sopherim, the doctors of the Law, controlled the future of Judaism.

CHAPTER XV.

Ezra the Sopher.

THE most distinguished of the sopherim, the very type and representative of his order, was a man who owes his fame rather to tradition than to history, but in whose case tradition is so consistent and emphatic that the high position claimed for him can scarcely be disputed. With Ezra, it has been said, one stands at the cradle of Judaism. In Jewish tradition he figures as a second Moses. His was the hand that gave a new and lasting shape to the least plastic of all materials that ever reformer had to work upon—the character of the Jewish people. He was the man of his age who set an indelible mark on succeeding ages. If Ezra's great reputation rested solely on what is told of him in the canonical books, his title to it might be called in question. He certainly appears in those books as a man of sincere piety, of unselfish patriotism and unbending firmness of will; but the actual outcome of his reforming energy does not seem very remarkable, even where he succeeded, which was not at every point of the line. It would be strange indeed if the comparatively narrow aims which history ascribes to this man had led to such broad results as appear in the whole future development of Judaism. Since the results are undeniably there, and since Jewish opinion is unanimous in attributing them to his influence and activity, one has to conclude that the meagre, disjointed notices of Ezra's career in the canonical books give a most inadequate conception of what he was and of what he did for his people. Those autobiographic and biographic fragments, which unfortunately are all that the Jewish chronicler saw fit to preserve, have to be read in the light of the verdict pronounced by posterity upon the man and his labours. They give a certain insight into Ezra's motives and methods, but they leave much untold.

Ezra belonged by birth to the priesthood—to the highest rank of the priesthood, for he traced his descent directly from Aaron through a long line of High Priests, of whom the last in his pedigree was Seraiah, the grandfather of Joshua ben Jehozadak. He was thus a Zadokite, a kinsman of the then High Priest at Jerusalem. This illustrious ancestry was enough in itself to make Ezra a notable man among his countrymen of the Golah; they spoke of him as 'the Priest'[1]—the chief representative in the land of exile of that powerful caste which still maintained its distinct character, though cut off from the exercise of all ritual functions. But it was not the high-priestly lineage of Ezra that constituted his main title to honour among the foreign Jews. It was his knowledge of the Torah, in which he excelled all other scholars of his time. At first distinguished as 'the Priest,' he became afterwards more highly distinguished by a title which really described his vocation—the title of 'Ezra

---

[1] Ezra vii. 11; x. 10, 16; Neh. viii. 2. In the Codex Alex., the apocryphal Book of Ezra is entitled simply ὁ ἱερεύς —*The Priest*. Neteler (*Bücher Esdras, etc.*, 39 refers the title 'chief priest' in Ezra vii. 5 not to Aaron but to Ezra himself; and supposes that the latter held an official or quasi-official position among the Babylonian Jews analogous to that held by Joshua and his successors among the Judeans. But it is most improbable that any such dual chief-priesthood ever existed, even in name.

the Sopher."[1] On the study of the sacred writings Ezra had brought to bear all the resources of a powerful intellect, working under the impulse of the strongest religious feelings. He was esteemed by his countrymen as an 'expert sopher of the Torah of Moses'[2]—as the foremost exponent of the new learning, the greatest living authority in this branch of knowledge, which was in truth all knowledge.

Tidings of the change of front that had been accomplished at Jerusalem, and of the consequent laxity now prevailing there in matters of religious observance, could not fail to reach the communities of the Golah. The lively interest which the foreign Jews had at one time taken in the fortunes of their brethren of the medinah, which had prompted them on several occasions to send delegates with gifts for the temple, seems to have grown comparatively languid and fitful in the course of years. The great distance that lay between them, the perils of the long journey, the political troubles of the time, had tended to produce a separation even in thought and

---

[1] Neh. viii. 4, 13; xii. 36. Ezra vii. 6.

sympathy between these two bodies of the people. Still, the inter-communication can never have been quite broken off. Pilgrimages of pious Jews to the land of their fathers and the temple of their God, though not yet the regular institution they afterwards became, were at least occasional; and those divided families, of which one part still dwelt in the East and the other in Judea, formed a bond of connection and a channel of intercourse between the Israel abroad and the Israel at home. In those circles of the Golah where now an intense spirit of devotion to the Law prevailed, reports of what was passing at Jerusalem were likely to raise other feelings besides that of strong disapproval. The Babylonian Jew, proudly conscious of his zeal for the Law, was inclined to look down on those who were satisfied with a lower standard of orthodoxy than his own. Babylon, the seat of Jewish learning, exalted itself above Jerusalem, where the Law was so little studied and its precepts so carelessly observed. It seemed as though the true centre of Judaism, instead of shifting to the mother-country, was now, and might continue to be, fixed on this side the River.

The days were past when any community of the Golah would dream of sending messengers to Jerusalem to inquire of the priests there concerning the Law;[1] they themselves had the knowledge now, and were fitted to teach those from whom they had formerly sought tuition. Their countrymen of Judea had the temple, the altar, the hierarchy; but experience had shown that their religion might exist independently even of the sacrificial system, and the sopher more than take the place of the priest. The zealots of the Torah might hold that 'to obey was better than sacrifice'— though not quite in the sense intended by the author of that phrase. The temple itself had been significantly named by the Exile-Prophet, not 'the house of sacrifice,' but 'the house of prayer.'[2] Houses of prayer might be set up elsewhere than at Jerusalem; already the Golah had, if not yet houses, at all events places of prayer, where the faithful people gathered to worship Jehovah and to hear His Word from the lips of their spiritual teachers. Thus the apparent indifference of the Baby-

---

[1] *Suprà*, p. 187.   [2] Isa. lvi. 7.

lonian and Persian Jews to the fate of the Palestinians may be accounted for, partly by the political difficulties in the way of giving help, but partly also by the growth of a feeling that even the Temple might be done without if only the Law were faithfully upheld at Babylon; that the mingling of Jewish with Gentile blood among the Judeans mattered comparatively little, so long as the Golah maintained that unblemished purity of race which was thought to justify the boastful saying of a later time, that 'all lands are dough compared with the land of Israel, and the land of Israel is dough compared with Babylon.'

Very different was the view taken by Ezra, when the news came to him of the falling away of the Jewish colony from that high ideal with which it had set forth from Babylon more than half-a-century ago. The thought that at Jerusalem the people were living in ignorance of the Torah, and their leaders setting it at nought, awoke in him a feeling of mingled sorrow and wrath and fear for the future. To Ezra belongs the credit of recognising the supreme importance of Jerusalem as the centre of Judaism at this stage of its development. Whatever opinion others might hold, it was in his judgment absolutely essential that the scattered Jewish race should have its spiritual metropolis, its holy city. It was not enough that the Law should be reverently studied and punctiliously followed at Babylon, so long as at Jerusalem it was either unknown or ignored. Judaism must have its 'local habitation;' 'out of Zion' must 'go forth the Law;' not only as to the place where for all Israel sacrifice was offered, but as to the place where for all Israel the Torah was studied and elucidated, and the example set of strict obedience to its ordinances, the Jews dispersed over the world must be able to look to Jerusalem. And there was another consideration which must have had great weight with one holding the convictions that Ezra held. At Babylon the Law might be observed faithfully, but it could not be observed completely. The legal prescriptions as to meats clean and unclean, purifications, dress, and so forth, might be carried out by the pious Jew in a foreign land: but there was in the Torah a great body of legislation relating to sacrifices and offerings, to the priesthood, to the festivals, which must remain a dead letter apart from Jerusalem and the Temple. In the view of Ezra and his school, the Torah must be taken as a whole; where every commandment had an equal authority, eclecticism was impiety; and as it was only at Jerusalem that Ezra could hope to realise his ideal of 'the Law, the whole Law, and nothing but the Law,' his thoughts and desires were drawn irresistibly thither. The dream of his life, the thing on which he had 'set his heart,'[1] was to be the teacher of Israel perishing for lack of knowledge. To equip himself for this mission he had not only made a profound study of the Law, but had been careful to carry out in his own practice the theory of unconditional obedience to its commands.[2] He had his own copy of the Law, the product of laborious years—a version more comprehensive than any that had been before, to which his great reputation gave unrivalled authority. With this Book in his hand,[3] Ezra was prepared to reform Israel, according to his own idea of reformation.

Ezra vii. 10.   [2] *Ibid.*   [3] Ezra vii. 14, 25.

He was well aware of the difficulties that lay before him. His Book of the Law was no talisman, the mere sight of which would overawe opponents and compel submission. Single-handed, he could not hope to deal effectively with the hostile influences that certainly awaited him at Jerusalem. He could not hope to arouse a people sunk in ignorance and apathy, and to overrule rulers who had made expediency and self-interest their guides. Ezra acted on his own maxim. He 'made many disciples.' He formed his school. There gathered round him a band of men like-minded with himself, animated with the same burning zeal for the Law, impressed with the same conviction that it must be taught at Jerusalem as at Babylon, and that in so teaching it they were carrying out the very purpose of the Eternal. At the head of such a company, Ezra might go forward to his task with some measure of confidence.

But before the first step could be taken in the enterprise, before any considerable number of the Babylonian Jews could migrate from one province of the empire to another, the consent of the Persian King had to be obtained. How long Ezra may have worked and waited for this is unknown. In all probability, nothing was attempted during the reign of Xerxes, which lasted twenty years. The character of that king forbade the hope of a successful appeal to him, and the Jewish patriots were little likely to hazard any move which would bring them and their people under the notice of the capricious tyrant. But in the year 465 B.C. a palace conspiracy removed Xerxes from the throne, and, as the result of a series of intrigues and assassinations, the succession devolved upon his youngest son, Artaxerxes I., called Longhand.[1] This prince is said to have been the handsomest man of his day, but the qualities of his mind by no means corresponded to those of his person. Weak, pliant, fond of ease, he allowed himself to be ruled by the women of his family, whose morals were of the worst, and who too often made an evil use of their influence over the king. Hitherto the Achæmenians had all been soldiers; even Xerxes, voluptuary as he was, had led his

---

[1] So called, according to the Greeks, from a physical peculiarity—because his right hand was longer than his left, or because his arms were so long that they reached to the knee. The by-name is probably figurative, referring to the world-wide extent of his sway.

armies in the field. But in Artaxerxes Longhand the martial spirit of his line seemed quite extinct. Peace, however inglorious, he preferred to the troubles and risks of war; and his timorous policy of coming to terms with enemies or rebellious subjects did much to hasten that decay of the Persian empire which had already set in under his predecessor on the throne. Yet this feeble, unwarlike king was perhaps more popular with his subjects than any other of his dynasty. Good-natured, approachable, averse from all cruelty or harsh use of his despotic power, Artaxerxes was looked upon as a model ruler by a people which had outlived the vigour of its youth and prime, and was now bent on enjoying the sweets of empire, forgetting that the sword must keep what the sword had won.

The natural amiability of Artaxerxes, the easy bonhommie which disposed him to shower his favours lavishly on all suitors,[1] may partly account for his indulgent treatment of the Jews. But the quite exceptional privileges he granted them, his apparently sincere

---

[1] A trait referred to by Plutarch, in his *Life* of Artaxerxes the Second.

anxiety for the proper establishment of their religion, point to impulses and springs of action lying deeper than mere careless good-nature. It is possible that, from the first, Jewish influence may have been powerful at the court of this king. Later in his reign a Jew is found holding an office which brought its occupant into most intimate relations with royalty, and was coveted by the noblest of the Persians for their sons. There may have been other men of Hebrew race besides Nehemiah who, in this as in previous reigns, stood near the person of the monarch, shared his confidence, and helped to bias his opinions. Jewish favourites at court had no doubt their share in obtaining the royal sanction for Ezra's proposed mission of reform; but the records of the time, lightly as they touch on this point, seem to show that other and more potent influences were at work for that end. The pious life and religious zeal of the Golah had not been without effect upon the nations among which they dwelt. Judaism had every-where its proselytes; 'from the rising of the sun even unto the going down of the same,' says the prophet who wrote in this period, the name of Jehovah was 'great among the Gentiles, and in every place incense and a pure oblation were offered' to that name.[1] Among those worshippers of the God of Israel there may have been Persians of the highest rank, grandees of the empire, officers of the household, who counted it a duty and a privilege to further the interests of Jehovah's people. The legend of Esther may perhaps be taken as indicating that Judaism had found its way into the seraglio of the Great King, as afterwards it found its way into the palace of the Cæsars. Nehemiah in his memoirs hints in passing [2] that Damaspia, the Queen-Consort of Artaxerxes, looked favourably on the Jews and their advocates at court. It has even been suggested that Artaxerxes himself may have been a worshipper of Jehovah,[3] and certainly the inference might fairly be drawn from the terms of the commission which he placed in Ezra's hands. But the Chronicler, who professes to give a copy of that document,[4] has evidently done so after a fashion of his own; and though there is no reason to doubt

---

[1] Mal. i. 11.
[2] Neh. ii. 6.
[3] Grätz, *Gesch*. ii. 128.
[4] Ezra vii. 11.

that such a document actually existed, or even that the Jewish transcript preserves the general sense of the original, one cannot but look with suspicion on passages in which, as has been said, the Persian king is made to speak 'like a born Jew.'[1] In the version of the Jewish copyist, Artaxerxes speaks of Jehovah as 'the God of heaven,'[2] and in the same breath as 'the God of Israel,' 'the God of Jerusalem,' and, in addressing Ezra, 'thy God'[3]—an obvious inconsistency which alone would make it reasonably doubtful whether this Gentile monarch ever thought or spoke of Jehovah as 'the God of heaven' at all. But though there is no real ground for supposing that Artaxerxes, even in secret, had exchanged the worship of Ormazd for that of Jehovah, it may quite well be that he was influenced by a certain superstitious reverence for the God of the Jews. From a statement in his memoirs,[4] it appears that Ezra had an audience of the Great King, in which he

---

[1] Grätz, *ibid.*
[2] Ezra vii. 12, 21.
[3] Ezra vii. 15, 19.
[4] These begin with the 27th ver. of chap. vii.

exalted the name of the Most High, and spoke with lofty confidence of His power to protect His servants and to punish His enemies.[1] One can imagine how a man of the stamp of Ezra—no prophet, but holding his convictions as firmly and uttering them as courageously as any prophet had ever done—might impress and dominate the mind of the feeble Artaxerxes, and make him eager to propitiate the God of the Jews by showing himself a benefactor to the Jewish people. Something of that fear of offending an unknown, foreign divinity, so characteristic of paganism, comes out in one passage of the royal missive—'for why should there be wrath against the realm of the king and his sons?'[2]

Three things Ezra needed for the successful accomplishment of the task he had set before him—men, money, and authority. The men were needed as an infusion of fresh blood into the home community. Ezra knew that he must have some leverage, some backing of public opinion, in his attempt to raise his people, and as this was not to be found in

---

[1] Ezra viii. 22.   [2] Ezra vii. 23.

Judea, he had to bring it with him from
Babylon. The money was needed to 'beautify
the house of Jehovah,'[1] to replenish the
Temple treasury, so that offerings might no
longer fail for the altar and revenues for
the priesthood. The authority was needed
to re-establish the supremacy of the Law
in face of all opposition. On all these
points the wishes of Ezra were satisfied to
the uttermost. He obtained leave to take up
with him to Jerusalem any of his people who
might freely join him, priests, Levites and
laymen, without restriction as to number
or class.[2] He was allowed to receive gifts
in money and in vessels for the Temple
from his countrymen in Babylonia, to which
the king himself and the members of his
council added a magnificent contribution.[3]
He was authorised to draw upon the king's
treasurers 'beyond the River,' for the uses
of the Temple and its hierarchy, to the
amount of a hundred talents of silver
(nearly £25,000), a hundred *kors* of wheat, a
hundred *baths* of wine, the same quantity of

---

[1] Ezra vii. 27.   [2] *Ibid.*, 13.   [3] *Ibid.*, 15-19.

oil, and salt at discretion.[1] An exceptional privilege was also, through his agency, conferred on the priesthood of Jerusalem. Henceforth, by royal ordinance, all ministrants of the Temple, from the chief priests down to the lowest Nethinim, were exempted from payment of taxes or tribute[2]—a concession which might be expected to help in smoothing the way for Ezra's intended reorganisation of the hierarchy.

These proofs of royal favour, however remarkable, were not a new thing in the experience of the Jews. Other Persian kings before Artaxerxes had allowed them to migrate homewards, had offered gifts for their Temple, and made provision for the maintenance of their worship. The novel feature of this edict of Artaxerxes was the position it assigned to a man of Jewish race, the authority it gave him over his countrymen. The nature and scope of that authority were of the most extraordinary character. Armed with these credentials, given under the hand and seal of the Great

---

[1] Ezra vii. 21, 22. The *kor* = about 44 imperial gallons; the *bath* = one-tenth of a *kor*.
[2] *Ibid.*, 24.

King, Ezra became the chief magistrate of his people, not merely in Palestine, but in Syria and Phœnicia, the land 'beyond the River.'[1] It was not, of course, intended that his jurisdiction should supersede that of the pekhoth and other officials of the crown in those regions. His province was exactly determined; he was to administer the Mosaic code—'the Law of his God which was in his hand.'[2] But as the Mosaic code, interpreted after the fashion of Ezra and his school, covered and regulated the whole life of the nation, civil and social as well as ecclesiastical, and was itself the fountain of all legitimate internal authority, the man who had power to enforce that code was really a dictator in Israel, held in check by nothing save his own reverence for the Law. Ezra had this power, so far as it could be conferred by a firman of a Gentile king. He was appointed Chief Judge, with authority to set subordinate magistrates and judges of his own choosing over the people. In one clause of the edict—perhaps the most singular passage in that singular document—the Torah of

---

[1] Ezra vii. 25.   [2] *Ibid.*, 14.

Moses was expressly declared to be henceforth, for all Jews, the same as a law of the Great King; and to Ezra, as a Persian official, was given the right of punishing any breach of the Torah as though it were a breach of the laws of the Medes and Persians, by fine, imprisonment or banishment, or even by death.[1] Ezra was not the man willingly to let such authority lie idle, or to shrink from pronouncing even the capital sentence if an example had to be made. Animated by a zeal quite equal to that of his ancestor Phinehas, unswerving in his fidelity to the one purpose and idea of his life, unflinching as to consequences—he was fitted by temperament to go to the bitterest extreme of persecution, and to play a terrible part in the history of his nation. That he made no use of the dangerous powers vested in him need not be taken as an evidence that such powers were never conferred, had never any existence save in the imagination of an admiring historian of a later time. Unquestionably he went up to Jerusalem as the plenipotentiary of the Great King, determined at

---

[1] Ezra vii. 26.

all costs to carry out his mission of reform.
But from the first his path was beset with
difficulties which obliged him to modify his
plans. He found that the boasted 'long arm'
of Artaxerxes lost in strength the further it
was stretched out, and that his edicts carried
much more weight at Susa or Babylon than in
the distant Syrian province. When that province became the seat of rebellion, Ezra's
authority fell with his master's, the weapon
with which he had been armed broke in his
hand; and afterwards he had to learn by bitter
experience that a king may change his mind,
and at the bidding of policy abandon those
whom he was pledged to protect. It is possible
that these crises and changes in the politics of
the Gentile world, adverse as they seemed at
the time, may have saved Ezra from com-
mitting a serious and perhaps irretrievable
error. But for these he might have attempted
to do by force what could only be done by
softer and subtler methods. But for these he
might have failed to realise that the despotism
of a Gentile ruler could never bring about in
Israel the great end he had set before him—
the spiritual despotism of the Law.

CHAPTER XVI.

The New Emigration.

EZRA received his credentials in the sixth year of Artaxerxes (460 B.C.), and at once set about preparing for his mission to Judea. The time seemed by no means propitious for a peaceful enterprise such as his. For in this sixth year of Artaxerxes, Egypt had again broken out in sudden and fierce revolt against the Persian monarchy, and the whole Trans-Euphratene must have felt the effects of the war which was raging on the Nile. The Egyptians, led by a chief who proclaimed himself the heir of the ancient Pharaohs, won a great battle in the Delta, in which the Persian satrap of Egypt was slain. An Athenian fleet brought powerful succour to the rebels; what remained of the Persian army of occupation was shut up in the citadel of Memphis; and it seemed as if the African province must be irrecoverably lost to the empire of the Great King. In this emergency Artaxerxes entrusted the command of a huge army, numbering, it is said, not less than half a million of men, to Megabyzus, satrap of Syria—a man who plays a not unimportant part in the Jewish history of this period, and whose after career had a very considerable influence on the fortunes of Ezra and his mission. Megabyzus was a kinsman of Artaxerxes by marriage, and had been actively concerned in the intrigues that raised that prince to the throne. His able generalship restored the credit of the Persian arms in Egypt. But his victories over the rebels and their Grecian allies proved in the end scarcely less damaging to the empire than previous defeats had been.

Undeterred by the threatening aspect of affairs 'beyond the River,' trusting in the edict of the Great King, and still more in 'the good hand of his God upon him'—a pious phrase much favoured by the Puritans of that day [1]—Ezra summoned his countrymen in

---

[1] Ezra vii. 9; *Cp.* vii. 6, 28; viii. 18; Neh. ii. 8, 18.

Babylonia to break up their peaceful homes, and go forth under his guidance from the land in which they had been settled for now a hundred and thirty years. He had already chosen out from among the Golah certain 'chief men'[1]—heads of distinguished Jewish families, belonging both to the priesthood and the laity, whose zeal for the Law and devotion to his person pointed them out as trustworthy supporters. By these family chiefs the invitation to join in this second Return was brought to the various communities of the Babylonian Jews. The place fixed upon for the mustering of the emigrants was on the banks of the Ahava, a stream unknown to geographers; possibly an affluent of the Euphrates, or one of the numerous canals fed from that river which crossed and recrossed the Babylonian plain.[2] Thither,

---

[1] Ezra vii. 28.

[2] Herzfeld (*Gesch.* ii. 14) supposes the starting-point of the expedition to have been somewhere in Susiana, not Babylonia. Grätz also (*Gesch.* ii. 128) suggests that the Ahava may have been a Persian river, and finds a possible connection between the name Casiphia (Ezra viii. 17) and that of the Choaspes, the well-known stream which flowed past Susa. But in Ezra vii. 6, viii. 1, it is distinctly stated that the starting-point was Babylon. The Jewish communities in Susiana and Media

on the appointed day—the first day of the first month of the seventh year of Artaxerxes (Nisan, March, 459 B.C.)—came a goodly number of the men of Israel with their wives and children, and pitched their tents beside the waters, ready for pilgrimage.

Three days were spent by Ezra in reviewing and numbering his followers.[1] Not less strict measures were taken now than at the time of the first Return in order to secure absolute purity of race in all who joined the enterprise. Each individual, before being recognised as an adherent, had to show his name enrolled in the register of his family; and in a formal document drawn up by Ezra's own hand[2] were recorded the genealogy of each family of the emigration, the name of its then head, and the number of its members. Of the laity there

---

may have sent contingents to the expedition (*cp.* Josephus, *Ant.* xi. 5, 2), but for the most part it was no doubt composed of Babylonian Jews.

[1] Ezra viii. 15.

[2] Ezra viii. 1-14. The family names in this list are, with very few exceptions, found in the list of the people who returned under Zerubbabel. The reference in ver. 13 to the 'last sons of Adonikam' does not mean that of this family the last members still remaining in Babylon now returned to Judea. 'Last' here probably = 'latest-born'; the reference being to the cadet branches of a family.

were in camp fifteen hundred men, all of flawless pedigree, representing the best blood of Judah. The number of the priests is not stated, but must have been considerable, for though Ezra names in his list only two priestly houses—those of Gershom and Daniel[1]—he refers elsewhere to twelve of their *sarim* or 'chiefs' as being set apart by him for a special service.[2] Among the laity was at least one scion of the stem of David. The priesthood comes first in Ezra's list, but immediately after it, in the place of honour at the head of the laity, stands the name of Hattush ben Shemaiah, a lineal descendant of Zerubbabel.[3] Including women and children, and the recruits who joined later,[4] the whole congregation numbered probably from 6000 to 8000 souls. This imposing assemblage on the Ahava proved how deep-rooted and wide-spread among the Jews in those foreign countries was the idea that they were a people set apart, whose hope for the future depended on their keeping apart from all others. It proved also how powerful

---

[1] Ezra viii. 2 ; see *suprà*, p. 60, note.
[2] *Ibid.*, 24.
[3] *Ibid.*, 2 ; cp. 1 Chron. iii. 22.   [4] Ezra viii. 18-20.

was the influence which Ezra wielded over his countrymen, and how implicitly they trusted in the leadership of the great Sopher.

Ezra's inspection of his followers brought to light one circumstance which caused him the gravest concern. In the whole encampment not a single Levite was found. The reasons which had made the sons of Levi so unwilling to join in the first Return [1] had evidently lost none of their force in the interval; they knew that the Zadokites had grasped all power at Jerusalem, and that their claim to parity of position in the church had small chance of being recognised. Ezra may have hoped that the privilege he had secured for them in common with the priesthood—the exemption from payment of taxes and tribute to the Persian crown—might tempt the Levites to join his enterprise. The result had disappointed him, but he was none the less resolved not to go up to Jerusalem without some representatives, at least, of the Levitical order in his train. It is not at all likely that Ezra had any purpose in his mind of playing off Levites against Zadok-

---

[1] *Supra*, p. 56.

ites, and using the aspirations of one section of the hierarchy as a means of breaking down the monopoly of power held by another.[1] His aim was to introduce the elements of reform, by means of new men, into every grade of the Temple *personnel*, from the highest to the lowest. And he was bent also on having his company complete in every part, as the emigration led by Zerubbabel and Joshua had been —the Jewish people in microcosm. He had with him the sons of Aaron; he had the laity arranged in twelve great family groups, typical of the twelve tribes of old;[2] he had a representative of the ancient royal house. The absence of the Levites left a gap in the ranks of Israel which must be filled up, at whatever cost of delay.

At a place, otherwise unknown, called Casiphia—either a town near Babylon, or perhaps a quarter of the great city itself—there was at that time an important settlement of Levites, which included also a large number of the descendants of the former Nethinim or

---

[1] Sack, *Altjüd. Religion*, 71.
[2] The names of twelve great families are mentioned in Ezra viii. 3-14—a number which can scarcely be accidental.

Temple serfs. The history of this period shows with what extraordinary tenacity the Jews in Babylon clung to the ties of family, and how steadfastly they maintained in exile those class distinctions which had grown up in their native land. Jewish society survived the fall of throne and temple, and the dissolution of the state. The political bonds had snapped, but the social bonds still held. It is therefore not incredible that in Ezra's day, even after the lapse of a hundred and thirty years, families of Levites should be found living together at one place; nor even that the Nethinim, whose forefathers had been 'given' as servants to the Levites, should preserve the tradition of their caste, and still own a certain allegiance to their hereditary masters. But this settlement of Casiphia seems to have been something more than a mere group of families drawn together by the ties of kinship or caste. Ezra, in his difficulty as to the Levites, chose out a formal deputation of twelve[1] men—two *mebinim* or 'teachers,' members of the new order of sopherim, and the rest 'heads' or chief men

---

[1] Probably, as Ewald (*Hist.* v. 138) suggests, one name has dropped from Ezra viii. 16.

of the people—and these, he says, 'I sent forth
unto Iddo, the head in the place Casiphia; and
I put words in their mouth which they should
speak unto Iddo and his brothers . . . that
they should bring us servants (*i.e.*, Levites) for
the house of our God.'[1] In what sense Iddo
bore the title of 'head' over the Jews at
Casiphia, what office he held, can only be conjectured. But it may be that this obscure
passage has reference to a school of Jewish
learning which had already sprung up at
Babylon—to a community or society of
Levites, bound together for the study of the
Law under Iddo as president.[2] If this were

---

[1] Ezra viii. 17. The text here is evidently corrupt. 'Iddo and his brothers' (Heb. 'brother') cannot themselves have been Nethinim, as in that case they would not have been at the head of a community of Levites. Neither can the passage read 'Iddo, and his brethren the Nethinim,' for the latter were not 'brethren' of the Levites by birth, in which sense only the term 'brethren' would be used. Nor is it to be supposed that the Levites themselves are referred to here under the name *Nethinim* or *Nethunim* ('given' to the sons of Aaron for the service of Jehovah; cp. Numbers iii. 9; xviii. 6); since in the Books of Ezra and Nehemiah the name is invariably used to describe the order of Temple serfs. Schultz (in Lange's *Bibelwerk, ad loc.*) suggests the reading:—'To Iddo, and to his brethren (the Levites), and to the Nethinim.'

[2] 'Was Casiphia the name of a college or institution, in which a large number of Levites resided and received their culture? Some provision must also have been made for the

so, it would explain why Ezra should have sent to Casiphia for the men he wanted. It would show also whence he derived most valuable assistance in his task of instructing the people.[1] And it might account for the fact that he asked Iddo to send him Levites, but not himself to join the emigration: the guild of scholarship at Casiphia could not spare its head, and Iddo's usefulness at Babylon was greater than it could be at Jerusalem. However this may be, Ezra's appeal was not made in vain. His deputies came back to the camp on the Ahava, bringing with them about forty Levites with their families, representing all three classes of the order, Levites proper, choristers, and Temple guards.[2] With them came also a considerable body of Nethinim.

The pilgrim train was now complete; it only remained to strike the tents, to load the beasts of burden, and begin the march homeward. But now, on the eve of departure, a certain feeling of anxiety, even fearfulness,

---

instruction of the Babylonian Jews, and it fell to the Levites by ancient usage to impart it.'—Bertheau-Ryssel, 104.

[1] Neh. viii. 7.
[2] Ezra viii. 18, 19; cp. vii. 7.

showed itself among the emigrants, as they thought of the many helpless women and children in their company, of the vast amount of treasure they were carrying with them, and then of the perils of the journey. Ezra makes allusion once and again to 'the enemy in the way,' to those that 'lay in wait by the way.'[1] Brigandage was always a flourishing institution in the Persian empire; even in the quietest times, even along the great roads which Darius had protected by forts and garrisons,[2] travellers were not always safe from the attack of wild tribes which lived by plunder, and set the imperial authority at defiance. The dangers of the journey which lay before Ezra and his caravan were probably increased by the circumstances of the time. The rebellion in Egypt had put a severe strain on the resources of the empire; the Syrian satrapy, in particular, through which lay the route to Judea, must have suffered from the disorders consequent on the withdrawal of Persian troops and their despatch to the seat of war. Ezra signifies that he might have had for the

---

[1] Ezra viii. 22, 31.   [2] Herod. v. 52.

asking a military escort, such as Cyrus had granted to the first emigration. But he had assured the king that the destinies of Israel were guided and guarded by a mightier Hand than that of the greatest of earthly monarchs; and now—though murmurs of disapproval and dismay might make themselves heard in the camp, though his own heart might sink for the moment at the thought of the many 'hostages to fortune,' for whose safety he was responsible—he was 'ashamed'[1] to go back upon these brave words, and to bring discredit upon the name of Jehovah among the Gentiles by confessing to a want of trust in His power or will to defend His servants. Better to face the risks of travel, to take their chance of escaping the banditti of the mountains or the desert, than to make the King believe that the spokesmen of the Jewish people were mere boasters, feigning a confidence they did not really feel. Ezra decided accordingly, and his decision showed true prudence as well as true faith. He proclaimed a fast on the Ahava. The whole

---

[1] Ezra viii. 22.

congregation humbled themselves before God, committed 'themselves, their little ones, and all their substance' to the divine protection.[1] Fortified by these exercises of religion, inspired by the calm courage of their leader, they put away their fears, and made ready to set out on the long and hazardous journey.

Having decided not to apply for an escort, Ezra had to make the best provision he could for the safeguarding of the treasure he was taking up with him to Jerusalem. This was of immense value. The Jews in Babylon and their Persian sympathisers had sent as an offering for the sanctuary six hundred and fifty talents of silver and a hundred talents of gold, together with twenty golden vessels worth a thousand darics, silver vessels worth a hundred talents, and two vessels of 'fine bright brass,' whose rarity made them precious as gold.[2] If the Chronicler's figures may be trusted, the specie and plate represented a sum of not less than half a million sterling. Ezra chose out a com-

---

[1] Ezra viii. 21, 23.   [2] Ezra viii. 26 27.

mission of twelve priests and twelve Levites,[1] and, having taken an exact inventory of the treasure, appointed them its custodians until it should pass into the proper hands at Jerusalem. It was not on the intrinsic value of the treasure that Ezra laid emphasis in exhorting its guardians to vigilance and fidelity, but on the fact that it was an offering for the Temple, and therefore 'holy to Jehovah.'[2] As such it was entrusted to the charge of 'holy men,' who must be ready to answer for its safety, if need were, with their lives.

On the twelfth day of the month Nisan[3] the pilgrims broke up their camp and began their march. Just seventy-eight years had passed since Zerubbabel led his countrymen homeward. Outwardly these two emigrations had certain features of resemblance. In both cases, starting-point and goal were the same; so also was the season of departure, the spring month of the year. In both cases permission to return had been granted by the favour of a Gentile

---

[1] Ezra viii. 24. 'Sherebiah, Hashabiah, and ten of their brethren with them' are Levites; *cp.* viii. 18, 19, 30. The 'even' of R. V. confuses the plain sense of the passage.
[2] Ezra viii. 28, 29.   [3] Ezra viii. 31.

king; in both the people went forth laden with costly gifts for the Temple, in offering which Gentile had vied with Jew; in both they were sped on their way by the prayers and good wishes of great bodies of their countrymen who remained behind. Both emigrations, though unequal in numbers, were alike in forming a complete representation of the Jewish people in all its classes and orders. But in spirit and temper the men who had gone up with Zerubbabel differed widely from those who now went up with Ezra. The former were enthusiasts. Their exultant joy, their unbounded hopefulness, were those of the captive whose prison-door has been newly thrown open and his fetters struck off; who has been newly led from the darkness and chill of the dungeon into the free air and warm sunshine. Signs and wonders had been wrought before their eyes. Marvels long foretold had come to pass in their experience. Other and still grander prophecies fired their imagination, and it seemed as if the overthrow of their enemies and their own deliverance were a presage of near fulfilment. Israel was to rise from the dust, more glorious than ever in the past; her sons were to step at once into their full inheritance; the Golden Age was to begin. In this sanguine spirit the first emigrants came back to their native land. Check upon check, failure after failure, shattered their illusions and quenched their enthusiasm. The soaring hopes and brilliant dreams were given up; the disappointed idealists sank into a mood of sullen depression, from which the spell of prophecy might rouse them for the moment, but which it could not charm away. From this sluggishness of religious feeling and this low tone of religious life had proceeded abuses which, in the eyes of Ezra and the men of his school, constituted a deadly peril for the future of Judaism. They believed that they knew and could apply the only remedy for these abuses. They, too, were zealots, but with a difference. They were under no illusion. They left Babylon knowing exactly what was the work that lay before them, and what was the life that awaited them in Judea. They had taken their resolve, not in an hour of exaltation, under the influence of fervid appeals and magnificent promises, but from sober conviction and a firm sense of duty, deliberately counting the cost and finding it not too high. The leader in their enterprise was a man of different mould from those whose feeble hands had hitherto misguided or failed to guide the destinies of the Judean colony. He was a man who had thoroughly made up his mind, who was never troubled by a doubt as to the rectitude of his motives or the justice of his methods; a Puritan of the Puritans, with all the defects of his qualities; hard, narrow, intolerant, but unquestionably strong. It was not to be expected that a reformer of Ezra's type, coming into the midst of such a state of society as that then existing at Jerusalem, would carry through his reforms easily and smoothly. Between the fiery zealot, the stern judge, with his Book of the Law as the one criterion of conduct, and the time-serving politicians, the astute men of the world who then ruled in Judea, a bitter conflict was certain to arise. Neither party might be able to claim a complete victory. But the very stir of such a conflict might prove sufficient in itself to give health and new life to the people.

BY THE SAME AUTHOR.

"THE STORY OF DANIEL: HIS LIFE AND TIMES."
3RD EDITION.

OPINIONS OF THE PRESS.

"The difficult task has been skilfully done. It has resulted in a graphic and vivid historical biography as engrossing as a volume of Macaulay; and proving that, whatever else there may be, there is at all events a warm interest in the ancient documents. If books like the 'Story of Daniel' were more common, modern faith in the flesh and blood reality of the Old Testament saints would not be so exclusively an intellectual effort as it now often is. . . . A clever, cultured, and interesting book."—SCOTSMAN.

"A second edition is published of the 'Story of Daniel' . . . an eloquent version of the Old Testament narrative, the details of which are illustrated and expanded by much historical and archæological knowledge."—SCOTSMAN.

"The author has done his work very thoroughly, laying under contribution a throng of writers, ancient and modern, and gathering into a focus the scattered rays of light which they send upon one of the dimmest periods of history. . . . This volume will occupy a place which there has hitherto been no English book to fill.—GLASGOW HERALD.

"He has taken advantage of all the side-lights, . . . has focussed them upon Daniel and his times, and produced a connected narrative that reads like a historical romance. Our perusal of this book has only deepened our first favourable impression of its merits."—DUNDEE ADVERTISER.

"It is almost needless in noticing a second edition of this book, to speak of its very excellent qualities. It is a scholarly work arranged in a thoroughly artistic style."—GLASGOW NEWS.

"A most picturesque narrative. As a historical monograph the book is worthy of the highest praise."—THE PRESBYTERIAN.

"The Life of the great Jewish Prophet and Politician is not often followed with such erudition and thoroughness of treatment as we discern in these pages."—BOOKSELLER.

"He has grasped the main features in the character and career of the prophet with penetrating insight, and he presents them to the reader with graphic force and felicity."—CHRISTIAN LEADER.

"That such a work could be in a very high degree useful, may be well conceived. As a compend of historical evidence it must prove of great service, not only to the preacher but also to the general reader."—HOMILETIC MAGAZINE.

"The various traits in the character of Daniel are beautifully depicted, and with the light which modern discoveries throw on the history of the past—of which the author has freely availed himself—the Book of Daniel becomes more real than ever."—CHRISTIAN TREASURY.

"Ministers in want of a theme that has not been at all over-discussed or preached out, should make the acquaintance of the book."—CHRISTIAN WORLD.

"A notable book upon the Life of Daniel. . . . Daniel will be a new Book to many after perusal of this work; we need more of such instruction."—SWORD AND TROWEL.

www.ingramcontent.com/pod-product-compliance
Lightning Source LLC
Chambersburg PA
CBHW030306240426
43673CB00040B/1082